PASSWORD 3

A Reading and Vocabulary Text

Lynn Bonesteel

Boston University

PEARSON
Longman

Password 3

Pearson Education, 10 Bank Street, White Plains, NY 10606

Executive editor: Laura Le Dréan
Development editor: Andrea Bryant
Marketing manager: Joe Chapple
Production editor: Helen B. Ambrosio
Senior manufacturing buyer: Dave Dickey
Photo research: Dana Klinek
Cover design: Tracey Munz
Cover photos: © Tom and Dee Ann McCarthey/Corbis; © Royalty-Free/Corbis; © Ed Young/Corbis
Text design: Ann France, Patricia Wosczyk
Production management and text composition: Elm Street Publishing Services, Inc.
Text font: 11/13 Palatino
Photo credits: See p. xiv
Illustration credits: Jill C. Wood and Elm Street Publishing Services, Inc.
Dictionary entries from *Longman Dictionary of American English*

Library of Congress Cataloging-in-Publication Data

Bonesteel, Lynn.
  Password 3 : a reading and vocabulary text / by Lynn Bonesteel.
     p. cm.
  Includes bibliographical references and index.
  ISBN 0-13-140893-3
 1. English language—Textbooks for foreign speakers. 2.
Vocabulary—Problems, exercises, etc. 3. Readers. I. Title: Password
three. II. Title.
PE1128.B623 2005
428.6'4—dc22

                    2004015191

ISBN: 0-13-140893-3

LONGMAN ON THE **WEB**

Longman.com offers online resources for teachers
and students. Access our Companion Websites, our
online catalog, and our local offices around the world.

Visit us at **longman.com.**

Printed in the United States of America
    6 7 8 9 -CRK- 08 07 06

Contents

Scope and Sequence

vi

INTRODUCTION

To the Teacher

The *Password* series is designed to help learners of English develop their reading skills and expand their vocabularies. Each book in the series offers theme-based units with engaging readings, a variety of activities to develop language skills, and exercises to help students understand, remember, and use new words.

Any book in the series can be used independently of the others. *Password 1* is for high beginners assumed to have an English vocabulary of about 600 words; *Password 2* assumes a vocabulary of about 1,000 words; and *Password 3* assumes a vocabulary of about 1,500. With each book, students will learn more than 400 new words and phrases, all of them high-frequency in American English. The *Password* series can help students reach the 2,000-word level in English, at which point, research has shown, most learners can handle basic everyday oral communication and begin to read unadapted texts. The vocabulary taught in the *Password* series has been carefully chosen. Target word choices have been based on analyses of authentic language data in various corpora, including data in the Longman Corpus Network, to determine which words are most frequently used and therefore most likely to be needed by students. Also targeted are common collocations and other multi-word units, including phrasal verbs. Most of the target vocabulary has been determined not by the topic of a chapter but rather by the frequency and usefulness of the words across a range of subjects.

While becoming a good reader in English does involve more than knowing the meanings of words, there is no doubt that vocabulary is key. To learn new words, students need to see them repeatedly and in varied contexts. They must become skilled at guessing meaning from context but can do this successfully only when they understand the context. For that reason, the sentence structure and vocabulary in the readings have been carefully controlled. The vocabulary used in the readings is limited to those 600 or 1,000 or 1,500 high-frequency words that the learner is assumed to know, plus the words and phrases to be targeted in the chapter and those recycled from previous chapters. The new vocabulary is explained and practiced in exercises and activities, encountered again in later readings and tasks, and reviewed in oral drills and self-tests. This emphasis on systematic vocabulary acquisition is a highlight of the *Password* series.

OVERVIEW OF *PASSWORD 3*

Password 3 is intended for intermediate students. It assumes a vocabulary of about 1,500 English words and teaches about 400 more. Between 14 and 20 words and phrases from each reading passage are targeted in the exercises for that chapter and recycled in later chapters. Because of the systematic building of vocabulary, as well as the progression of reading skills exercises, it is best to do the units and chapters in the order in which they appear in the book.

Most of the target words are among the 1,500 highest-frequency words in English—the vocabulary that students need to build a solid foundation in English. Occasionally, somewhat lower-frequency words have been targeted for their usefulness in discussing a particular theme. For example, the third unit, "The Science of Genetics," includes the target words *gene* and *trait,* and the fifth unit, "Man and Beast," includes the target words *chimpanzee, domestication,* and *socialize.*

Organization of the Book

The book contains six units, each with three chapters followed by a Wrap-up section. After Units 3 and 6, there are Vocabulary Self-Tests. At the end of the book, you will find the Index to Target Words and Phrases.

UNITS   Each unit is based on a theme and includes three chapter readings and one reading in the unit Wrap-up. All of the reading passages deal with real people, places, ideas, and events. Students need to understand the content, and they need to speak and write about it.

CHAPTERS   Each of the three chapters within a unit is organized as follows:

Getting Ready to Read   Each chapter opens with a photo or illustration and two types of pre-reading questions or tasks—first a speaking and then a vocabulary exercise. The speaking activity in *Getting Ready to Read* starts students thinking about the subject of the reading by drawing on what they already know and eliciting their opinions. The vocabulary activity in *Getting Ready to Read* presents four to six of the target words in context. This activity serves to reduce the vocabulary load of the reading passage itself, while at the same time serving as a preview of some of the central ideas of the reading.

Reading   This section contains the reading passage for the chapter. These passages progress from about 500 to about 800 words by the end of the book. Students should do the reading the first time without dictionaries. You may wish to have them reread while you read aloud, as listening while reading can be helpful to students' comprehension and retention. It is also helpful for students to hear the pronunciation of new words. The reading is followed by *Comprehension Check,* a true/false/? (can't determine the answer from the text) exercise that lets students check their general understanding. It is a good idea to go over the *Comprehension Check* statements in class. When a statement is true, you may want to ask students how they know it is true; when it is false, have students correct it. By doing so, you send them back into the reading to find support for their answers. Try to avoid spending time explaining vocabulary at this point. Assure students that they will have ample opportunity to learn the new words in subsequent exercises.

Exploring Vocabulary   This section begins with *Thinking about the Vocabulary.* First students learn and practice a *Guessing Strategy* that helps them develop their ability to guess the meaning of unfamiliar words from context. Next students are asked to look at the list of Target Words and Phrases and circle (both on the list and in the reading) those that are new to them. Then they reread, noticing the uses of these particular words, and using the guessing strategy wherever possible. They may need to work on this first as a whole class, with your guidance; later they can discuss new word meanings in pairs. *Using the Vocabulary* follows, with an exercise to help students understand the meanings of the target vocabulary as used in the reading. When taken as a whole, *Using the Vocabulary* is actually a summary of the most important information from the text. This exercise can be done in class or out, by students working individually or in pairs.

Developing Reading Skills   Once students have a better understanding of the meaning of the target vocabulary, they engage in a variety of tasks that help them become better readers. The exercises in this section include work on reading for topics, main ideas, major points and details; scanning; summarizing; understanding inference; understanding reference words; understanding cause and effect; understanding the writer's purpose; recognizing the writer's tone and point of view; and paraphrasing.

Expanding Vocabulary   In this section, students move from understanding the target vocabulary to actively acquiring it. First they practice using the target words in new contexts. Then they build on their knowledge of the target vocabulary by learning related items that are in the same word families. Finally, they complete a word grammar, phrasal verb, or word collocation exercise. Grammar exercises include using *due to, because,* and *so;* using transitive and intransitive verbs; the proper use and placement of adverbs; participial adjectives; transitive verbs and direct objects; using *used to;* adjectives that become nouns with *the;* reflexive pronouns; and gerunds and infinitives. Phrasal verb exercises provide students with practice in using common phrasal verbs. Word collocation exercises focus students' attention on how the target words combine with other words.

Only after working through all the exercises in *Expanding Vocabulary* should students turn to their dictionaries for further information.

Putting It All Together   This section includes activities to help students consolidate their understanding of the unit theme, build their fluency, and continue their acquisition of the target vocabulary. In the *Discussion* section, students are asked to share information and opinions about issues raised in the chapter. In some cases, they are asked to conduct surveys on topics related to the chapter theme. As they talk, they are instructed to use the target vocabulary (including derived forms that were introduced in the chapter). The words that are most likely to be useful to each discussion item are listed with the questions for easy reference. You may want to specifically assign someone from each group to keep track of how many times the words were used in the discussion. At the end of the discussion, you can ask the class which words or phrases they used the most, and provide additional instruction on any vocabulary they had difficulty using.

The chapter ends with a *Writing* section containing a choice of two topics related to the content of the reading. Students are instructed to use at least five of the target words in their writing. You can encourage them to choose words or phrases that they need to learn more about. Some of the writing tasks lend themselves to informal writing such as journal entries or letters, while others are more appropriate for formal compositions and short essays. How you wish to use them will depend on the specific writing tasks, as well as your goals for the course.

UNIT WRAP-UPS   Each unit ends with a four-part Wrap-up section that provides students with more practice in the reading skills and vocabulary taught in the three chapters. The first section, *Reviewing Reading Skills and Vocabulary,* includes a 300 to 400-word reading passage related to the unit theme, with 10–20 target words and derivations from the unit incorporated into the text. Each passage also contains a few new vocabulary items to give the students practice in guessing meaning from context. The follow-up exercises provide the students with additional practice in the reading skills introduced in the unit.

The other three sections of the Wrap-up provide a key follow-up to the initial learning of the vocabulary—to consolidate and enrich students' understanding of new words. The second section of the Wrap-up, *Expanding Vocabulary,* contains exercises on word families, phrasal verbs, grammar, and collocations. The third section, *Playing with Words,* includes a crossword, word search puzzle, or game; and the fourth, *Building Dictionary Skills,* contains exercises designed to help students get the most out of their dictionaries, with excerpts from the *Longman Dictionary of American English.*

VOCABULARY SELF-TESTS   Two multiple-choice vocabulary tests appear in the book, the first covering Units 1–3, the second Units 4–6. The answers are given at the back of the book, as these are intended for students' own use. (Unit tests can be found in the Teacher's Manual.)

TEACHER'S MANUAL

The Teacher's Manual for *Password 3* contains:

- The Answer Key for all exercises in the book
- Six Unit Tests with answers
- *Quick Oral Review,* sets of prompts you can use for rapid drills of vocabulary studied in previous chapters. These drills can be an important part of the spaced repetition of vocabulary—repeated exposures to newly-learned words at increasing intervals—that helps students remember the words they learn. For tips on how to use the prompts, see the Introduction in the Teacher's Manual.

To the Student

Welcome to *Password 3!* This book will help you improve your reading in English and expand your English vocabulary. The articles in it are about real people, events, ideas, and places from around the world. I hope you will enjoy reading, writing, and talking about them.

Lynn Bonesteel

About the Author

Lynn Bonesteel has been teaching ESL since 1988. She is currently a full-time senior lecturer at the Center for English Language and Orientation Programs at Boston University in Boston, Massachusetts.

References

Ackerman, T. "A brave new world of designer babies: Genetic engineering to open Pandora's box of ethical questions." *The Houston Chronicle*, (June 27, 1999): A1. [electronic version].

Alvarez, L. "Consumers in Europe Resist Gene-Altered Foods." *The New York Times*, (February 11, 2003): A3. [electronic version].

Anderson, W.F. "A cure that may cost us ourselves." *Newsweek*, (January 1, 2000): 74. [electronic version].

Blow, K. "Kurtis Blow Presents: The History of Rap, Vol. 1: The Genesis. (n.d.)." Retrieved January 1, 2003 from http://rap.about.com/gi/dynamic/ offsite.htm?site=http%3A%2F%2Frhino.com%2FFeatures%2Fliners%2F72851lin.html

Bowles, S., C. Jones & E. Poitevent. "An instant of anger…a lifetime of regret." *USA Today*, (November 23, 1998): A19. [electronic version].

Burr, C. *The Emperor of Scent: A Story of Perfume, Obsession, and the Last Mystery of the Senses.* New York, NY: Random House, 2002.

Chandler, D. "Ancient note: Music as bridge between species." *The Boston Globe*, (January 5, 2001): A1. [electronic version].

Dayton, T. "Rapper's Delight: The history of hip hop at Yerba Buena Center." *San Francisco Weekly*, Calendar, (May 16, 2001). [electronic version].

Gross, T. "Grandmaster Flash discusses his music and career." *WHYY Fresh Air*, (December 26, 2002). [electronic version].

Henig, R.M. "Tempting fates." *Discover*, 5, (May, 1998): 58–64. [electronic version].

Hughley, M. "Godfather of hip-hop DJs." *The Oregonian*, [Arts and Living], (July 5, 2002): 35. [electronic version].

Jackson, J. "Teens: Crazy by Design." *Ottawa Citizen*, (May 17, 2003): G1. [electronic version].

McElhenny, J. "Franklin Park Gorilla Escapes, Attacks 2." *Boston Globe*, (September 29, 2003): A1. [electronic version].

Patterson, K. "Road Rage: Scientists want to find out what makes a driver go bad." *Calgary Herald, Sunday Edition,* (July 7, 2002): A3. [electronic version].

Reader's Digest. "Drugs Get Personal." *Medical Breakthroughs 2001: The Latest Advances in Preventing, Treating, and Curing Nearly 100 Common Diseases.* Pleasantville, NY: Reader's Digest Association, 2002.

Seltz, Johanna. "Teen Brains Are Different." *The Boston Sunday Globe,* (May 28, 2000): E1.

Solomon, R.C. "Some Notes on Emotion, 'East and West'." *Philosophy East and West,* 45, (1995): 171–202. [electronic version].

Turin, L. "Flexitral Odorants by Design. Rational Odorant Design. (n.d.)." Retrieved June 24, 2004 from www.flexitral.com/index.html

Who Named It. (n.d.). "How Listening to a Milkmaid's Story Can Change the World." Retrieved June 24, 2004 from http://www.whonamedit.com/doctor.cfm/1818.html

Acknowledgments

I would like to first thank Dr. Jeong-wha Choi, who graciously agreed to allow me to use her story. I would also like to thank Samuela Eckstut for being so generous with her time, advice, and encouragement.

I would also like to thank the reviewers whose comments on early drafts of this book were very helpful: **Christina Cavage,** Atlantic Cape Community College, Atlantic City, NJ; **Leslie Corpuz,** Tidewater Community College, Virginia Beach, VA; **Anthony Halderman,** Cuesta College, San Luis Obispo, CA; **Martha Hall,** The New England School of English; **Steve Horowitz,** Central Washington University, Ellensburg, WA; **Susan Jamieson,** Bellevue Community College, Bellevue, WA; **Kathy Sherak,** San Francisco State University, San Francisco, CA; **Julie Un,** Massasoit Community College, Brockton, MA; **Jo Dee Walters,** formerly affiliated with San Diego State University, San Diego, CA.

I'd also like to extend my gratitude to Linda Butler, whose vision and concept for the series were a constant source of guidance and inspiration as I worked on this project. Her feedback on the manuscript was also invaluable.

A great many people at Longman helped in the making of this book, most of all Executive Editor Laura Le Dréan and Development Editor Andrea Bryant. I would also like to extend my thanks to Associate Acquisitions Editor Lucille Kennedy, Production Editor Helen Ambrosio, Project Editor Amber Allen, Photo Researcher Dana Klinek, and Artist Jill C. Wood.

Finally, I would like to thank Claudia for always being there to remind me of what is important.

Text Credits

Photo Credits

UNIT 1
ARTISTIC INNOVATIONS

Pablo Picasso. Les Demoiselles d'Avignon. *1907. Oil on canvas.*

CHAPTER 1

What Is Anime?

Anime

Cartoon

GETTING READY TO READ

 Talk with a partner or in a small group.

1. Did you watch cartoons or read comic books when you were a child? Which ones? Do you ever watch cartoons or read comic books now? Which ones?

2. Compare the picture labeled "Anime" and the picture labeled "Cartoon" above. Check (✓) the words that you think describe the pictures. Explain your answers to your classmates.

	beautiful	creative	intelligent	funny	serious	interesting	simple
Anime	■	■	■	■	■	■	■
Cartoon	■	■	■	■	■	■	■

B The **boldfaced** words in the sentences below appear in the reading. Which words are new to you? Circle them. Then, work with a partner. Read the sentences about the reading, and choose the correct answers.

1. Some of the best, most **talented** artists in Japan work in anime. Someone who is *talented*

   a. has a lot of money.   **b.** has a very good natural ability.

2. Anime deals with **complex** characters and situations. The stories are usually not simple. A *complex* story

   a. has many parts and is difficult to understand.   **b.** usually has a sad ending.

3. In most Hollywood films, it is easy to tell who is good, and who is bad. The **evil** characters do bad things, and the good ones try to stop them. An *evil* character wants to

   a. hurt other people.   **b.** meet other people.

4. Both children and adults are **fascinated** by anime, and enjoy watching it together. *Fascinated* means

   a. very surprised.   **b.** very interested.

5. Some anime deals with the future and the changes that **technology** might bring to people's lives. Examples of *technology* include

   a. schools, banks, and museums.   **b.** computers, digital cameras, and cell phones.

READING

Read the text once without stopping. Don't worry about new words or the numbered words at the bottom of the page. Don't stop to use a dictionary. Just keep reading!

What Is Anime?

1   *Anime* is a special style of Japanese animation.[1] You can immediately see the difference between anime and other cartoons. This is because of the high quality of the artwork and the style, such as characters with large, childlike eyes. In addition, you will see that anime is strongly influenced by Asian, and especially Japanese, religious and cultural traditions. It provides a window into Japanese culture.

continued

_____

[1] *animation* = a movie or television program made by photographing pictures or by drawing a series of pictures with a computer

2   Anime is closely **related** to Japanese comics called *manga*. Many anime television shows and videos **got their start** as popular manga. Manga is a $3 billion business in Japan. About 60 percent of all printed materials sold there are manga. And manga and anime are not just for children. They are popular with Japanese of all ages. In fact, a large percentage of manga and anime is made for adults only. Their **popularity** helps explain why the quality of anime is so high—anime and manga are big business. A recent anime film **reportedly** cost $8 million to make, with more than three thousand animators **involved** in its production. Some of Japan's most **talented** artists and musicians work in manga and anime.

3   But it is not just the quality of the artwork that makes anime so popular. Many anime stories deal with **complex** subjects and characters that change as the stories develop. The "bad guy"[2] of Disney[3] cartoons—completely **evil** and not very believable[4]—is not common in anime. Rather, it is not always clear who the "good guys" and "bad guys" are. Also, death is shown as a natural part of life. Even important characters die sometimes. If your only experience with animation is Disney, you might feel shocked but then **fascinated** when you first watch anime.

4   Some of the most interesting anime deals with modern **technology**. In this type of anime, the differences between machines and people, males and females, and good and evil are not always clear. Anime often looks at the **challenges** of life and culture in a world of **rapid** technological change. The characters in this type of anime deal with deep **moral** questions, such as the possible negative effects of technology on human relationships. This is very different from the simple way that Hollywood films and cartoons usually deal with the same subjects.

5   In Japan, anime appears in three forms: television shows (which often continue for several years), **original** animation video (OAVs, also spelled OVA), and films. The first Japanese anime TV show, *Tetsuawan Atom* ("The Mighty Atom"), started in 1963 and continued for ten years.

6   Anime is becoming popular in countries all over the world. For people who do not speak Japanese, videos are available that have subtitles[5] added or are dubbed.[6] Many people greatly prefer the subtitles, for a number of

continued

---

[2] the *bad guy* = the character in a movie, book, or television show that does bad things and that you are supposed to hate

[3] *Disney* = a U.S. company famous for making cartoons, such as Mickey Mouse, and cartoon movies, such as *The Lion King*

[4] *believable* = easy to believe because it seems possible and real

[5] *subtitles* = words printed at the bottom of a movie screen to translate what is said by the actors in a foreign movie

[6] *dubbed* = a **dubbed** movie or video is one in which the original sound recording is replaced with one in another language

reasons. Sometimes the dubbing is either too fast or too slow, so what you hear does not match the mouth movements. Also, hearing the spoken (and sung) Japanese is part of the cultural experience and **beauty** of anime. Perhaps most importantly, many anime viewers are learning a little Japanese as they watch.

7   Funny, fascinating, intelligent—these are some of the adjectives that describe the best anime. If you share anime with children, you will be sharing with them beautiful art, excitement, and lots of fun. You will also be introducing them to the fascination of Japanese culture. In fact, families around the world who watch anime find that their children fall in love with Japan and the beautiful Japanese language.

Comprehension Check

Read these sentences. Circle T (true) or F (false). If you circle F, change the sentence to make it true. You might need to change one or two words, or you might need to rewrite the sentence completely. Check your answers with a classmate. If your answers are different, look back at the reading.

different
1. Anime and Disney cartoons look very ~~similar.~~   T   Ⓕ

2. Manga is a special kind of anime.   T   F

3. A lot of anime is made especially for adults.   T   F

4. Anime often deals with very serious subjects.   T   F

5. Important characters never die in anime.   T   F

6. It is possible to enjoy anime even if you don't speak Japanese.   T   F

EXPLORING VOCABULARY

Thinking about the Vocabulary

Guessing Strategy

Learning how to figure out what a new word means is a very important skill. In every chapter of this book, you will learn a strategy to help you guess the meaning of a word from its **context**. The context of a word is the words and sentences before and after it. These other words help you to guess a word's meaning. For example, look at the context of the word *complex* in the example.

Many anime stories deal with **complex** subjects and characters that change as the stories develop. The "bad guy" of Disney cartoons—completely evil and not very believable—is not common in anime. Rather, it is not always clear who the "good guys" and "bad guys" are.

The context tells you that something that is complex changes and is not always clear. Therefore, complex subjects and characters are not simple.

Try It!

Read the sentences, and write a definition of the **boldfaced** target word.

The **popularity** of anime is growing. Millions of people all over the world are starting to watch it.

Popularity means _____

Look at the target words and phrases. Which ones are new to you? Circle them here and in the reading. Then read "What Is Anime?" again. Look at the context of each new word and phrase. Can you guess the meaning? Use the Guessing Strategy where possible.

Target Words and Phrases

related (paragraph 2)	involved (2)	fascinated (3)	moral (4)
got their start (2)	talented (2)	technology (4)	original (5)
popularity (2)	complex (3)	challenges (4)	beauty (6)
reportedly (2)	evil (3)	rapid (4)	

Using the Vocabulary

These sentences are **about the reading**. Complete them with the words and phrases in the box. Circle the words or phrases in the sentences that help you understand the meanings of the target words.

beauty	challenges	got their start	involved	moral
original	popularity	rapid	related	reportedly

1. Anime is closely _____ to Japanese comic books. They are connected because they have some of the same characters and a similar style of artwork.

2. Many anime television characters first appeared in the pages of popular comic books, and then later on television. They _____ in comic books.

3. Anime is popular with people of all ages in Japan. Because of its
   _____, anime is big business in Japan.

4. According to newspaper reports, anime films usually cost millions of
   dollars to make. One recent film _____ cost $8 million to
   produce.

5. Many talented Japanese artists and musicians are _____ in the
   making of anime. Over 3,000 artists worked on a recent anime film.

6. The stories in anime are complex, and the characters often have to deal
   with difficult _____ challenges. In anime, the differences
   between good and evil and right and wrong are often not very clear.

7. Because of technology, life is changing very fast, and many people have
   difficulty accepting all the changes. Some of the most interesting anime
   deal with the _____ of living in a world of _____
   change.

8. People enjoy watching anime because of its artistic quality and
   _____.

9. A lot of anime is made first for film and television, and then later appears
   on video. However, _____ animation video, or OAV, is made
   directly for video, not first for film or television.

DEVELOPING READING SKILLS

Understanding Topics and Main Ideas

A reading is about someone or something. That person or thing is the **topic** of
the reading. Often, the title of a reading will tell you what the topic is. The
main idea of a reading is the most important information about the topic. The
main idea of a reading is usually written in a full sentence.

Answer these questions.

1. What is the topic of "What Is Anime?" _____
   _____

2. What is the main idea of "What Is Anime?"
   a. Anime is a form of Japanese animated film or video that is artistic, fun, and
      educational.
   b. Anime got its start in Japan as manga, or comic books, and is very popular.
   c. Anime is better than Disney animation because the characters are more complex.

Understanding Cause and Effect

When you read, it is important to understand the connections between ideas. For example, you must be able to tell the difference between the cause of something and the effect. Often, writers use words like *so, because,* and *therefore* to show cause and effect, but sometimes they do not.

Complete these sentences using information from "What Is Anime?"

1. Makers of anime spend a lot of money producing it because <u>anime is</u> <u>big business in Japan.</u>

2. Anime is very popular because _____

    _____

3. When people who watch only Disney cartoons first watch anime they might be shocked because _____

    _____

4. Many people don't like to watch anime that is dubbed because _____

    _____

5. Many children who watch anime want to learn Japanese because _____

    _____

EXPANDING VOCABULARY

Using the Vocabulary in New Contexts

These sentences use the target words and phrases **in new contexts.**
Complete them with the words and phrases in the box.

beauty	challenges	got his start	involved	moral
original	popularity	rapid	related	reportedly

1. The president is _____ traveling to China tomorrow. That's what I read in the newspaper this morning, anyway.

2. She has faced many difficult _____, but she has always been successful.

3. Parents have a _____ responsibility to teach their children right from wrong.

4. The owner of this restaurant _____ as a waiter here.

5. Because of the musician's _____, he was paid $250,000 to play one show.

6. That is not the _____ painting. It's a copy.

7. Many people think that we are sisters, but we are not _____.

8. We were all _____ in the discussion, but our boss made the final decision.

9. His English is good, but he still has trouble understanding

   _____ speech.

10. She visits Costa Rica every year because she loves the natural

   _____ of the rain forest.

Word Families

Many words belong to **word families.** When you learn a new word, it is a good idea to learn other words in the same family. Use your dictionary to check the form and meaning of words in the same word family.

   The words in the exercise below belong to the word families of the target words. You will see that they have different endings, or **suffixes.** A suffix is a word part added to the end of a word to make a new word. The new word is often a different part of speech.

- *-ity* is a noun suffix
- *-al* is an adjective suffix
- *-ly* is an adverb suffix

Complete the sentences with the words below.

morally	originality	popularity	rapidly	technological

1. The most important _____ inventions of the past 100 years include the airplane, the automobile, and the computer.

2. His _____ as a singer lasted for only a few years. Now, almost no one remembers him.

3. Technology is changing very _____ these days. It seems there are new products every day.

4. Stealing is _____ wrong.

5. I love the _____ of your work. It is different from everyone else's.

Studying Collocations

Collocations are words we often put together. **Prepositions** (for example, *in, on, of, to*) often go together with adjectives. Some prepositions can go with certain adjectives, and some cannot. Look at the examples.

Correct: He is not **related to** her.
Incorrect: He is not related with her.

A Read these sentences. Pay attention to the boldfaced words and the prepositions that go with them.

1. My son is <u>**fascinated** by</u> cars. He can tell you the name of almost every car he sees.

2. He didn't decide alone. Many people were <u>**involved** in</u> the decision.

3. Dogs are closely <u>**related** to</u> wolves. A long time ago, there were no dogs, just wolves.

4. She's very <u>**talented** in</u> music. Someday, she would like to be a famous musician.

B Write four sentences about yourself or people that you know. Use the **boldfaced** adjectives + prepositions from Exercise A.

1. _____

_____

2. _____

_____

3. _____

_____

4. _____

_____

PUTTING IT ALL TOGETHER

Discussion

Share your ideas in a small group. As you talk, try to use the vocabulary below. Each time someone uses a target word or phrase, put a check (✓) next to it.

beauty	complex	involve
original/originality	talented	

1. The writer of "What Is Anime?" refers to anime as art. However, when many people think of art, they think of famous artists such as Leonardo da Vinci or Pablo Picasso. Do you agree with the writer that anime and other types of animation can be considered art? Why or why not?

2. The writer says that anime "provides a window into Japanese culture." Think about the comic books, animated films, videos, or television shows that are made in your country. What could a foreigner learn about your culture from reading or watching them? If you are Japanese, talk about why you agree or disagree with the statement.

Writing

Complete one or both of these writing topics. When you write, use at least five of the target words from the chapter. Underline the target words in your paper.

1. Write a paragraph or short essay describing a comic book or cartoon character that you liked when you were a child. Explain why you liked the character.

2. *Comic books and cartoons can be considered art.* Do you agree or disagree with this statement? Write a paragraph or short essay explaining your opinion. Use examples of specific comic books or cartoons.

CHAPTER 2

The Scientist and the Stradivarius

Dr. Joseph Nagyvary analyzing an 18th-century violin

GETTING READY TO READ

 Talk with a partner or in a small group.

1. Do you play a musical instrument? If so, which one? How long have you been playing? If you don't know how to play a musical instrument, would you like to learn? Which instrument would you choose?

2. The text you are going to read is about a problem from the past that someone is trying to solve with modern science. What other problems from the past have modern science and technology been able to solve? What are some problems that scientists today are trying to solve?

B The **boldfaced** words in the paragraph below appear in the reading. Which words are new to you? Circle them. Then, work with a partner. Read this short summary of the reading, and match the words with their definitions.

Joseph Nagyvary is a scientist. He has spent many years trying to solve the **mystery** of why the eighteenth-century violins made by Antonio Stradivari sound so much better than other violins. Nagyvary has used his **knowledge** of chemistry to try to understand the **heavenly** Stradivarius sound. He believes that the **chemical** qualities of the materials used to make the violins have an effect on the sound. People who sell Stradivarius violins at very high prices feel **threatened** by Nagyvary's ideas. They do not want the mystery to be solved.

Word	Definition
_____ **1.** mystery	**a.** information gained through learning or experience
_____ **2.** knowledge	**b.** worried that something bad will happen to hurt you
_____ **3.** heavenly	**c.** (coming from) the changes in or qualities of a liquid, solid, or gas
_____ **4.** chemical	**d.** beautiful or good
_____ **5.** threatened	**e.** something that we don't know much about

READING

Read the text once without stopping.

The Scientist and the Stradivarius

1   When Regina Buenaventura walks onto the stage, all eyes are on her violin. In the fifth row, Joseph Nagyvary closes his eyes and listens. He has spent years in a **laboratory** studying the sound of the most famous instrument of all time. Nagyvary believes that he has finally solved the centuries-old **mystery** behind the **remarkable** sound of the Stradivarius violin.

2   This young musician holds the result of Nagyvary's scientific efforts under her chin—the Nagyvarius. She begins playing and the violin makes a clear, **brilliant, heavenly** sound. Creator Nagyvary opens his eyes. Could this be the magical Stradivarius sound?

3   For 150 years, violin makers, musicians, and scientists have tried to solve the mystery of the Stradivarius. Antonio Stradivari lived in Cremona, a small northern Italian city. Before his death in 1737, he made over 1,000

continued

violins, violas,[1] cellos,[2] and guitars. Two sons followed him into the business, but they died soon after. The details of how their father and other violin makers from Cremona made their remarkable instruments disappeared with them.

4   How could an **illiterate** man with no education produce instruments with such a heavenly sound? Did Stradivari and the other violin makers from Cremona have a secret?

5   Joseph Nagyvary's laboratory in the United States at Texas A&M University is a world away from Cremona. Nagyvary began teaching biochemistry[3] at the university in the late 1960s. About ten years later, he began making violins. Using his **knowledge** of chemistry, Nagyvary believes that he has found the answer to the Stradivarius puzzle.

6   In 1977, Nagyvary presented the results of his research to the Violin Society of America. He claimed that the high quality of Stradivari's instruments was not **due to** his **artistic** talent. Rather, the remarkable sound was a result of the materials Stradivari used, specifically the **chemical** properties[4] of the wood and varnish.[5] Stradivari himself probably did not understand the importance of these materials. In other words, Stradivari was certainly talented, but he probably owed much of his success to luck.

7   Nagyvary's **announcement** shocked violin makers and dealers.[6] His **theory** was a direct challenge to the way that violins had been made for years. It also challenged violin makers' **belief** in the importance of their artistic talent.

8   Nagyvary **stands by** his theory. "The pieces of the puzzle have been around and I have not invented anything new. But I put the pieces well together while the others could not. I am the first chemist of good international standing[7] . . . who, obviously, has a much better understanding of the effects of these natural chemicals."

continued

---

[1] a *viola* = a wooden musical instrument shaped like a violin but larger and with a lower sound

[2] a *cello* = a large wooden musical instrument, shaped like a violin, that you hold between your knees and play by pulling a bow (= special stick) across wire strings

[3] *biochemistry* = the scientific study of the chemistry of living things

[4] a *property* = a quality that belongs naturally to something

[5] a *varnish* = a clear liquid that is painted onto wood to protect it

[6] a *dealer* = someone who buys and sells a particular product, especially an expensive one

[7] *standing* = someone's position in a system or organization, based on what other people think of him or her

9   The best **proof** of Nagyvary's theory may be the instruments he makes. By using what he has learned from his research, Nagyvary claims to produce violins with a sound quality very similar to that of a Stradivarius. This is demonstrated in *The Stradivarius Puzzle,* a 13-song CD recorded by well-known professional violinist Zina Schiff. On it, Schiff plays both a Nagyvarius and her 1697 Stradivarius, reportedly worth $3,000,000. Schiff says, "I sent the *Stradivarius Puzzle* to a friend of mine who is a conductor[8] and he had no idea . . . He just could not tell . . . The truth is, I would rather be playing on one of Dr. Nagyvary's instruments."

10   So why do violin makers and dealers refuse to even discuss Nagyvary's theory? Schiff believes that it is because the dealers are **threatened** by the fairly low cost ($3,000 to $22,000) of a Nagyvary violin.

11   Schiff came from a poor family, so she feels very strongly that people who cannot afford Stradivari violins should still be able to have high quality instruments. According to Schiff, Dr. Nagyvary's violins have made this possible, without having a negative effect on the beauty and value of a Stradivarius.

---

[8]a *conductor* = someone who stands in front of a group of musicians and directs their playing

Comprehension Check

Read these sentences. Circle T (true), F (false) or ? (can't determine the answer from the reading). If you circle F, change the sentence to make it true. You might need to change one or two words, or you might need to rewrite the sentence completely. Check your answers with a classmate. If your answers are different, look back at the reading.

1. *thinks he knows*
    Dr. Nagyvary ~~is not sure~~ why Stradivari instruments   T   (F)   ?
    sound so good.

2. Dr. Nagyvary is both a scientist and a violinist.   T   F   ?

3. Dr. Nagyvary is both a university professor and a violin   T   F   ?
    maker.

4. According to Dr. Nagyvary, the chemicals in the wood and   T   F   ?
    varnish of Stradivari instruments are not very important to
    the way they sound.

5. According to Dr. Nagyvary, Stradivari knew why his violins   T   F   ?
    had such a remarkable sound.

6. Nagyvary violins sound better than Stradivari violins.   T   F   ?

EXPLORING VOCABULARY

Thinking about the Vocabulary

Guessing Strategy

If the unfamiliar word is an adjective (a word that describes a noun), think about whether it has a positive (good) or negative (bad) meaning. Look at the example.

> I will never forget the first time that I heard the **remarkable**, clear sound of a Stradivarius.

Because the writer describes the sound as clear (a positive quality), you can guess that the adjective *remarkable* probably has a positive meaning.

Try It!

Find these target words in the reading. Do they have a positive or a negative meaning? Write **P** (positive) or **N** (negative).

artistic _____   brilliant _____   illiterate _____

Look at the target words and phrases. Which ones are new to you? Circle them here and in the reading. Then read "The Scientist and the Stradivarius" again. Look at the context of each new word and phrase. Can you guess the meaning? Use the Guessing Strategy where possible.

Target Words and Phrases

laboratory (1)	heavenly (2)	artistic (6)	belief (7)
mystery (1)	illiterate (4)	chemical (6)	stands by (8)
remarkable (1)	knowledge (5)	announcement (7)	proof (9)
brilliant (2)	due to (6)	theory (7)	threatened (10)

Using the Vocabulary

These sentences are **about the reading**. Complete them with the words and phrases in the box. Circle the words or phrases in the sentences that help you understand the meanings of the target words.

announcement	artistic	beliefs	brilliant	due to	illiterate
laboratory	proof	remarkable	stands by	theory	

1. Dr. Joseph Nagyvary is a scientist who works out of his _____ at Texas A&M University.

2. Antonio Stradivari could not read or write. He was _____.

3. Stradivari violins have a very special sound. Dr. Nagyvary has spent many years of his life trying to solve the mystery of why they have such a _____ sound.

4. Stradivari violins make a sound that is so clear and _____ that it shines like a light.

5. Dr. Nagyvary believes that the high quality of Stradivari's instruments was not a result of his _____ talent. Rather, Dr. Nagyvary claims that the remarkable sound was _____ the materials Stradivari used.

6. Dr. Nagyvary made an _____ about his discoveries during a speech to the Violin Society in 1977.

7. Violin makers and dealers were shocked. Dr. Nagyvary's _____ challenged every tradition of violin making.

8. If Dr. Nagyvary is right, then a lot of what violin makers have always believed is wrong. His theory challenges all of their _____ about what is important in violin making.

9. Many people do not agree with Dr. Nagyvary's theory, but that doesn't bother him. He _____ his theory because he is sure that he is right.

10. One way that Dr. Nagyvary is trying to prove his theory is by making his own violins. Many professional musicians cannot tell the difference between his violins and Stradivari violins. Dr. Nagyvary claims that this is clear _____ that his theory is correct.

DEVELOPING READING SKILLS

Understanding Topics and Main Ideas

Answer these questions.

1. What is the topic of "The Scientist and the Stradivarius"? _____

   _____

2. What is the main idea of the reading? (Remember, a main idea must be written in a full sentence.) _____

   _____

Scanning

Sometimes you need to find a piece of information in a reading. To do this, you **scan** the reading. *Scan* means to read rapidly and look for just the information you need.

Read these questions about "The Scientist and the Stradivarius." Scan the reading and write short answers.

1. In addition to violins, what other kinds of instruments did Stradivari make?

   _____

   _____

   _____

2. Was Stradivari the only violin maker from Cremona who made instruments with a remarkable sound?

   _____

   _____

   _____

3. When did Dr. Nagyvary first make a speech about his theory?

   _____

   _____

   _____

4. How many and what kind(s) of violins does Zina Schiff play on *The Stradivarius Puzzle*?

   _____

   _____

   _____

Understanding Inference

Some information cannot be found by scanning. This is because the information is not written directly in the text. Instead, you have to think about what the text says, and then make a logical conclusion, or **inference**.

Answer these questions.

1. According to Dr. Nagyvary, Stradivari never told anyone his secret because

   a. he didn't know he had a secret.   **b.** he wanted to be famous.

2. Traditionally, violin makers believed that the most important thing in violin making was

   a. their own artistic talent.   **b.** the materials they used.

3. Stradivari's sons and other violin makers from Cremona made violins using

   a. the same kinds of materials that Stradivari used.   **b.** different kinds of materials than Stradivari used.

EXPANDING VOCABULARY

Using the Vocabulary in New Contexts

These sentences use the target words and phrases **in new contexts**. Complete them with the words and phrases in the box.

| announcement | artistic | belief | brilliant | due to | illiterate |
| laboratory | proof | remarkable | stand by | theory | |

1. My grandfather never learned how to read and write. He was _____.

2. _____ the bad weather, our flight arrived late.

3. You can't be sure that he stole the money. You don't have any _____.

4. Everyone thought that he loved his job. We were all shocked by his _____ at the meeting that he was going to quit.

5. Anna got her start working in a research _____. Then she decided to go to medical school.

6. Due to my father's strong _____ in the importance of education, he has decided to give $1 million to help illiterate people learn how to read and write.

7. It doesn't matter what my children do. I feel that I have a moral responsibility to _____ them.

8. My son showed _____ talent at a young age. He painted this beautiful picture when he was only ten years old.

9. A _____ is an idea or a set of ideas that explain something about life or the world.

10. This essay is _____. It is one of the most original essays I have ever read.

11. Look at the _____ color of those roses. I've never seen such a bright red.

Word Families

As you saw in Chapter 1, a suffix can tell you if a word is a noun, adjective, or adverb. Pay attention to suffixes. They contain a lot of information. However, remember that not all words have suffixes.

A Study the chart and answer the questions.

Noun (person)	Noun (skill, field, or activity)	Verb	Adjective
announcer	announcement	announce	
artist	artistry		artistic
chemist	chemistry		chemical

1. Which two suffixes show that a word refers to a person? _____, _____
2. Which two suffixes show that a word refers to a skill, field, or activity? _____, _____
3. Which two suffixes show that a word is an adjective? _____, _____
4. Which word in the chart does not have a suffix? _____

B Complete the sentences with words from the chart. Be careful; you will not use all the words.

1. Who told you? Did he _____ it, or did his boss?

2. The radio _____ lost his job because he made too many mistakes when he was reporting the news.

3. She is a famous _____. The museum just bought some of her paintings.

4. That _____ company develops products that are used in making new drugs.

5. He studied _____ in college, and now he works for a company that develops new drugs.

6. To be a good designer, you need both technical skill and _____.

Studying Word Grammar

There are many words and phrases that describe why something happens. Look at the sentences from the reading.

- He claimed that the high quality of Stradivari's instruments was not **due to** his artistic talent.
- Schiff believes that it's **because** the dealers are threatened by the fairly low cost ($3,000 to $22,000) of a Nagyvary violin.
- Schiff came from a poor family, **so** she feels very strongly that people who cannot afford Stradivari violins should still be able to have high-quality instruments.

Due to, because, and *so* all explain why something happens. However, the grammar that follows each one is different. *Due to* is followed by a noun or a noun phrase. *Because* is followed by a full clause (subject + verb). *So* is also followed by a full clause, but it introduces an effect, or result, rather than a cause. Also there is always a comma in front of *so*.

Ⓐ Complete these sentences with *due to, because,* or *so*.

1. She is successful _____ she has worked hard.

2. Her success is _____ her hard work.

3. She has worked hard, _____ she is successful.

4. _____ a family emergency, Frank will not be in this afternoon.

Ⓑ Write three sentences about your life. Use *due to, because,* and *so*.

1. _____

_____

2. _____

_____

3. _____

_____

PUTTING IT ALL TOGETHER

Discussion

Share your ideas in a small group. As you talk, try to use the vocabulary below the question. Each time someone uses a target word or phrase, put a check (✓) next to it.

1. What are some of the ways that artists such as painters, musicians, and dancers use technology in their work?

artistic/artistry	brilliant	due to	knowledge	remarkable

2. Imagine that you are a group of scientists and musicians, and you have to interview Dr. Nagyvary. Your goal is to find out more about his theory and how and why he developed it. Make a list of the questions you will ask him.

announce/announcement	artistic/artistry	belief	brilliant
chemical	due to	knowledge	laboratory
proof	remarkable	theory	threatened

Writing

Complete one or both of these writing topics. When you write, use at least five of the target words from the chapter. Underline the target words in your paper.

1. Write a paragraph or short essay describing a mystery that you would like to see scientists solve. Imagine how science could be used to solve the mystery.

2. Imagine that you are Dr. Nagyvary, and write a letter to a newspaper defending your theory. Use the questions that you and your group wrote for question 2 in the **Discussion** section above as a guide.

The History of Rap

DJ Grand Master Flash

GETTING READY TO READ

 A **Talk with a partner or in a small group.**

1. What kind of music do you like? What kind of music don't you like? Who is your favorite musician or singer?

2. Do you like to sing? Have you ever sung or done some other type of performance (for example, acting or dancing) in front of people? If so, tell your partner about it.

3. Look at the chapter title and the photo. Write three questions that you think the reading will answer.

   a. When did rap music first become popular?

   b. _____

   c. _____

   d. _____

23

B The **boldfaced** words below appear in the reading. Which words are new to you? Circle them. Then, work with a partner. Read the definitions of the words, and complete the sentences next to each picture with the words.

equipment = the special tools, machines, etc. that you need for a particular activity or type of work

spinning = turning around and around very quickly

scratched = made a thin mark on a hard surface with something sharp or rough

performer = an actor, musician, dancer, etc., whom people watch

1. She is a _____.

turntable

2. The record is _____ on the turntable.

3. The DJ just _____ the record.

4. The DJ has a lot of musical _____.

READING

Read the text once without stopping.

The History of Rap

1   Rap is a spoken form of musical **expression**. It involves words spoken in **rhyme** with a recorded or **live** rhythm section.[1] Many people use the terms "hip hop" and "rap" to mean the same thing. In fact, hip hop is the culture that modern rap **grew out of**. Hip hop is a culture with its own language, clothing styles, music, and ways of thinking, and it is constantly growing and changing. It includes several different art forms, including visual art,[2] dance, and music. Rap is just one part of hip-hop culture.

2   Although there is a lot of disagreement about exactly where and how rap began, most people agree that it got its start in the mostly African-American[3] neighborhoods of the Bronx in New York City in the 1960s. At that time, large outdoor street parties called *block parties* were becoming popular. Young people who could not afford expensive musical instruments or **equipment** took simple turntables[4] and microphones[5] out onto the streets. But instead of just playing the music, they moved the **spinning**, or turning, records with their hands. At the same time, they **scratched** them with the needles of the turntables. The changes in the sound of the music became known as *cutting* or *scratching*. The young people who played the music were called *disc jockeys*. These disc jockeys, or *DJs,* used their turntables as instruments to create a new musical form.

3   Other **performers** working with the DJ **interacted** with the crowd by talking louder than the music, often in rhyme. These performers were called *emcees,* or *MCs,* and their interaction with the crowd became known as *rapping*. Later, the MCs became known as *rappers*. Interaction between the performers and the crowd is an important **characteristic** of rap.

4   Among the many people who **contributed** to the development of rap, artist Grandmaster Flash **stands out**. The **techniques** he invented have become an important part of hip-hop culture. Flash was one of the first DJs

continued

----

[1] a *rhythm section* = the part of a band that provides a strong beat using drums and other similar instruments

[2] *visual art* = art such as painting that you look at

[3] an *African-American* = an American with dark brown skin, whose family originally came from the part of Africa south of the Sahara Desert

[4] a *turntable* = the round flat surface on a record player that you put records on

[5] a *microphone* = a piece of equipment that you hold in front of your mouth when you are singing, giving a speech, etc., in order to make your voice sound louder

to begin using a turntable as a musical instrument, rather than just a piece of equipment that played records. First, he would find a short section of a song that he liked. This was called the *break*. Then he would use two copies of the same record and two turntables to invent creative ways to play the break over and over without stopping.

5   In the 1970s and 1980s rap's popularity grew, and the rhymes became more complex and **clever** as the performers **competed** with each other. The music that they rapped to included recordings of famous African-American musicians and breaks from popular disco[6] and rock music of the time. Many rappers also performed with live musicians.

6   Today, hip-hop culture is popular all over the world, and young people everywhere listen to rap. There are many reasons for rap's popularity. It offers young people the chance to express themselves freely. It is an art form that can be performed without a lot of money, training, or equipment. Rapping involves verbal[7] skills that many people already have or can develop. You can rap slowly, or you can rap fast. All of this allows rappers with very different **personalities** to express themselves.

7   This does not mean that rapping is easy, however. It **calls for** a quick mind, an ability to use language well, originality, and an excellent sense of rhythm.[8] It presents the performer with many challenges, but only two rules: rhyme to the beat of the music, and be original.

---

[6] *disco music* = a type of dance music with a strong repeating beat that was first popular in the 1970s

[7] *verbal* = spoken, rather than written

[8] *rhythm* = a regular repeated pattern of sounds or music

Comprehension Check

Read these sentences. Circle T (true) or F (false). If you circle F, change the sentence to make it true. You might need to change one or two words, or you might need to rewrite the sentence completely. Check your answers with a classmate. If your answers are different, look back at the reading.

                      culture

1. Hip hop is a ~~kind of music~~.   T   Ⓕ

2. Many people confuse rap and hip hop.   T   F

3. Rap got its start in Africa.   T   F

4. The first rappers didn't have a lot of money.   T   F

5. Rappers do not perform to live music.   T   F

6. To be a good rapper, you need to be able to use language in an original way.   T   F

EXPLORING VOCABULARY

Thinking about the Vocabulary

Guessing Strategy

The signal word *or* can help you guess the meaning of unfamiliar words. Look at the examples.

> But instead of just playing the music, they moved the **spinning**, or turning, records with their hands.

> Young people could not afford expensive musical instruments or **equipment**.

In the first sentence, *or* shows that what follows it—*turning*—means the same thing as *spinning*. In the second sentence, *or* shows that the word that follows it—*equipment*—is different in meaning from *musical instruments*. To determine what meaning the word *or* signals, look carefully at the punctuation. If there are commas around *or* and the word(s) following it, the meaning is similar. If there are no commas, the meaning is different.

Try It!

Read the sentences, and write a definition of the **boldfaced** target words.

1. Rappers can perform to **live** or recorded music.

Live means _____

2. One of raps' **characteristics**, or special qualities, is that the performers speak to the beat of the music.

Characteristic means _____

Look at the target words and phrases. Which ones are new to you? Circle them here and in the reading. Then read "The History of Rap" again. Look at the context of each new word and phrase. Can you guess the meaning? Use the Guessing Strategy where possible.

Target Words and Phrases

expression (1)	**spinning** (2)	**characteristic** (3)	**clever** (5)
rhyme (1)	**scratched** (2)	**contributed** (4)	**competed** (5)
live (1)	**performers** (3)	**stands out** (4)	**personalities** (6)
grew out of (1)	**interacted** (3)	**techniques** (4)	**calls for** (7)
equipment (2)			

Using the Vocabulary

These sentences are **about the reading**. What is the meaning of each **boldfaced** word or phrase? Circle a, b, or c. Then circle the words or phrases in the sentences that help you understand the meanings of the target words.

1. Rap is a special type of musical **expression**. Rap performers show their personalities through their music. *Expression* means

    a. something you say, write, or do that shows what you feel.

    b. an instrument that you play with great feeling.

    c. something that is becoming very popular.

2. Rap involves words spoken in **rhyme**, like in some poems. *Rhyme* means

    a. a very loud or very soft voice.

    b. two words ending in the same sound, like "hit" and "sit."

    c. a slow, soft, musical sound like "shhhh."

3. Hip-hop culture existed before rap, so we can say that rap **grew out of** hip-hop culture. *Grew out of* means

    a. had an effect on.

    b. developed from.

    c. created.

4. Rap artists **interact** with the crowd. The crowd shouts things out, and the performers answer them in rhyme. *Interact* means

    a. argue.

    b. communicate.

    c. sing.

5. In fact, crowd and performer interaction is one of the **characteristics** of rap. *Characteristics* means

    a. important problems.

    b. fastest parts.

    c. special qualities.

6. Grand Master Flash **contributed** a lot to the development of rap. *Contributed* means

    a. sang.

    b. gave.

    c. spent.

7. Grand Master Flash wasn't the only person who was involved in rap's development, but his work **stands out**. It was very important to rap's popularity. *Stands out* means

   a. is clearly better.

   b. is much harder.

   c. is a lot faster.

8. Flash invented a **technique** that involved using two turntables as musical instruments. *Technique* means

   a. special way of dancing.

   b. machine to make music.

   c. special skill that needs to be learned.

9. Rappers are good at using language, so their rhymes are often very **clever**. *Clever* means

   a. fast and difficult to understand.

   b. unusual and interesting.

   c. loud and funny.

10. Rap artists **compete** with each other to make the best rhymes. *Compete* means

    a. try to be stronger than someone else.

    b. try to be better than someone else.

    c. try to be kinder than someone else.

11. Every rapper has a different way of performing. That's because each rapper has his or her own special **personality** and way of expressing himself or herself. *Personality* means

    a. person who helps them in their work.

    b. people who like their way of performing.

    c. character and way of behaving.

12. Rapping is not easy. It **calls for** many different skills. *Calls for* means

    a. teaches.

    b. achieves.

    c. needs.

13. Sometimes rappers perform to **live** music, and sometimes they perform to recorded music. *Live* means

    a. performed with many singers or musicians.

    b. performed for people who are watching.

    c. performed in a new or different way.

DEVELOPING READING SKILLS

Scanning

A Where is the information about these topics in "The History of Rap"? Scan the reading, and write the paragraph number (1–7).

  _3_   **a.** MCs and rappers

_____ **b.** how rap and hip hop are related

_____ **c.** the development of rap in the 1970s and 1980s

_____ **d.** why rap is popular

_____ **e.** Grand Master Flash's contributions to rap

_____ **f.** how rap got its start

_____ **g.** the challenges of rap

B Write a sentence or two about each of the seven topics from paragraphs 1–7. Use information from the reading, but do not copy. Use your own words.

Paragraph 1. _Hip hop is a culture that includes several different art forms._
Rap is just one part of hip-hop culture.

Paragraph 2: _____

_____

Paragraph 3: _____

_____

Paragraph 4: _____

_____

Paragraph 5: _____

_____

Paragraph 6: _____

_____

Paragraph 7: _____

_____

Understanding Topics and Main Ideas

Answer this question.

What is the main idea of "The History of Rap"? Write a full sentence.

_____

EXPANDING VOCABULARY

Using the Vocabulary in New Contexts

These sentences use the target words and phrases **in new contexts.**
Complete them with the words and phrases in the box.

calls for	characteristics	clever	competing	contributes
expression	grew out of	interact	live	personality
rhyme	stands out	technique		

1. I love his _____. He's so clever, funny, and kind.

2. We need somebody really special for this job. The job _____ someone who is artistic, smart, and ready to work hard.

3. Police officers who work in big cities have to _____ with all different kinds of people every day.

4. He is one of the most brilliant students I've ever had. He really _____.

5. That artist uses a special _____ to make his colors look very bright.

6. What a _____ idea! You have a great imagination.

7. Stories for very young children are often written in _____. Little children like them because they sound like songs.

8. The two brothers are always _____ for their parents' attention. It's really sad.

9. She _____ about $1,000 a year to a children's hospital.

10. She plays the piano with wonderful _____. She hasn't been playing for a long time, but she knows how to communicate her feelings through her playing.

11. One of the most important _____ of a musical performer is talent.

12. It is much more exciting to go to a _____ performance than to watch it on TV.

13. His desire to become an artist _____ his fascination with color as a child.

> ### Word Families
>
> In Chapters 1 and 2, you learned that the suffixes *-ity, -try,* and *-ment* show that a word is a noun, and the suffixes *-er* and *-ist* show that a word is not only a noun but also a person. Other common suffixes for nouns are *-ion, -tion,* and *-ance.* Often, these suffixes are added to verbs to change them to nouns.

A **Add the correct suffix to make the noun form. Use your dictionary to check your answers.**

Verb Form	Noun Form
express	
perform	
interact	
compete	
contribute	
fascinate	

B **Complete the sentences with the nouns from Exercise A.**

1. He's usually a great actor, but his _____ in that movie was not very good.

2. Our team won the _____.

3. I think that babies should have _____ with a lot of different kinds of people instead of only their mothers or fathers.

4. Your _____ to the work of the team was very important. Thank you!

5. She wrote him a poem as an _____ of her love.

6. I don't understand your _____ with cars. What is so interesting about them?

Studying Phrasal Verbs

Stand out and **call for** are **phrasal verbs.** Phrasal verbs have two or more parts: a verb (such as *stand* or *call*) and one or more particles (such as *out* or *for*). The meaning of a phrasal verb is different from the meaning of just the verb alone. In Chapter 2, you learned the phrasal verb *stand by.*

Rewrite the underlined part of these sentences using the phrasal verbs *stand by, stand out,* and *call for.* You may need to change the form of the verb to fit the sentence.

1. Many of the musicians have some talent, but only two of them <u>are really remarkable</u>. _____

   _____

2. If you really believe in something, you should <u>defend</u> it. _____

   _____

3. That job <u>requires</u> someone who is very strong. _____

   _____

PUTTING IT ALL TOGETHER

Discussion

Work in a small group.

1. Ask each other these questions about music. Have one person write down everyone's responses. Decide who enjoys music most and who enjoys it least. Tell the class a few of the most interesting things you found out about each other.

   a. How many CDs (or cassettes or records) do you buy a year?

1. 0–5	**2.** 6–15	**3.** 16–25	**4.** more than 25

   b. How much time on average do you spend listening to music every day?

1. none or almost none	**2.** about 15 minutes	**3.** 30 minutes	**4.** an hour or more

   c. How many CDs (or cassettes or records) do you own?

1. fewer than 10	**2.** 11–30	**3.** 31–50	**4.** more than 50

   d. How many concerts do you go to a year?

1. none	**2.** 1 or 2	**3.** 3–5	**4.** 6 or more

e. Check all of the statements that are true for you.

_____ I listen to music while I study or work.

_____ I listen to music when I feel sad.

_____ I listen to music when I feel happy.

_____ I like to dance when I listen to music.

_____ I listen to music when I want to relax.

_____ Listening to music helps me fall asleep.

f. How often do you get music off the Internet?

1. never   **2.** rarely   **3.** sometimes   **4.** often

2. The reading describes rap in a very positive way. However, although rap is very popular in many parts of the world, there are some people who really don't like it. In fact, older people often do not like music that is popular with younger people. Why do you think this is true? Discuss your ideas. Try to use the vocabulary below the question in your discussion. Each time someone uses a target word or phrase, put a check (✓) next to it.

characteristic   compete/competition   contribute/contribution

express/expression   interact/interaction   live

performer/perform/performance   personality

Writing

Complete one or both of these writing topics. When you write, use at least five of the target words from the chapter. Underline the target words in your paper.

1. Choose a type of music that you like, and do some research on it (either at the library or on the Internet). Then, write an essay about it. Your essay should include the following information:

- A description of the music (for instance, the instruments used)
- The history of this type of music (where, when, and how it got its start)
- Well-known performers of this type of music
- Why you like it

2. Imagine that you have the opportunity to interview a famous performer (living or dead). Make a list of at least ten questions that you would like to ask during the interview.

Wrap-up

REVIEWING READING SKILLS AND VOCABULARY

Read the text. Do not use a dictionary.

1   Among the many talented artists of the twentieth century, Spanish painter Pablo Ruiz Picasso stands out. Due to his brilliant talent and originality, he is considered by many to be the most important artist of his time.

2   Picasso was born in 1881 in Málaga, Spain. His father was an art teacher, and he knew very early that his son Pablo was remarkably talented. At the age of 14, Picasso entered the Academy of Fine Arts in Barcelona, Spain. In one day, he completed the entrance test that traditionally took students a month to finish.

3   From 1900 to 1904, Picasso lived in both Spain and France. During that time, he worked in a completely original style, which became known as his Blue Period. The name came from Picasso's use of only the color blue in his paintings of the time. In 1904, Picasso moved to France, where he began working in a variety of modern artistic styles.

4   One of Picasso's many contributions to the history of art was the invention of the artistic technique of collage—using materials such as letters, cloth, or pieces of newspaper to make a piece of art. He was also involved in the development of cubism—a new style of modern art in which people and things are painted using shapes such as triangles and squares. In fact, many people consider Picasso's 1907 painting *Les Demoiselles d'Avignon* the first cubist painting.

5   Picasso's popularity today might make one forget that throughout his lifetime, he challenged Western European artistic traditions. Picasso died in 1973, but the beauty, complexity, and originality of his artistry live on in the many works he left behind.

Comprehension Check

Read these sentences. Circle T (true), F (false), or ? (can't determine the answer from the reading). If you circle F, change the sentence to make it true.

1. Picasso had a great influence on modern art.   T   F   ?

2. Picasso's father taught him how to paint.   T   F   ?

3. *Les Demoiselles d'Avignon* was painted during Picasso's Blue Period.   T   F   ?

4. Picasso was not the only painter to contribute to the development of cubism.   T   F   ?

5. Picasso did most of his work in a traditional style.   T   F   ?

Guessing Meaning from Context

Answer this question.

What is the meaning of *Academy* in paragraph 2?

_____

Understanding Inference

Check (✓) the sentences that you can infer from the text. Remember, an inference is not written directly in the text. You have to think about what the text says, and make a logical conclusion.

_____ 1. Picasso began to paint before the age of 14.

_____ 2. In his lifetime as a painter, Picasso used the color blue more than any other color.

_____ 3. Collage is a technique that is still used by artists today.

_____ 4. Picasso was not a popular artist when he was alive.

_____ 5. Picasso knew how to paint in a traditional style.

Scanning

Scan the reading to find the information to complete the sentences.

1. Pablo Picasso is considered one of the greatest painters of modern times because _____

   _____.

2. The years from 1900 to 1904 were called Picasso's Blue Period because

   _____

   _____.

3. *Les Demoiselles d'Avignon* is a very important painting because

   _____

   _____.

4. Picasso's contributions to art did not end with his death because

   _____

   _____.

EXPANDING VOCABULARY

Studying Phrasal Verbs

As you learned in Chapter 3, a **phrasal verb** has a verb and one or more particles. *Stand by* and *stand out* are phrasal verbs. It is often difficult to figure out the *exact* meaning of a phrasal verb, but you can get a *general idea* of the meaning by thinking about the meaning of the verb and the particle(s). The context will help you gain a more complete understanding of the meaning.

 Read these sentences. Match the phrasal verbs to their definitions.

1. Why are you just **standing around**? Don't you have any work to do?
2. His name is Philip J. Johnson. The "J" **stands for** his middle name, Jackson, which was his grandfather's name.
3. I don't understand why you let him treat you so badly. Why don't you **stand up for** yourself?
4. He's my boss. I don't like the way he treats me, but if I **stand up to** him, I might lose my job.

Phrasal Verb	Definition
____ 1. stand around	**a.** support or defend a person or idea that is being attacked
____ 2. stand for	**b.** refuse to accept bad or unfair treatment from a person or organization
____ 3. stand up for	**c.** stand somewhere and not do anything
____ 4. stand up to	**d.** represent a word, name, or idea, especially in a short form

B **Write your own sentences with the phrasal verbs from Exercise A.**

1. _____

   _____

2. _____

   _____

3. _____

   _____

4. _____

   _____

Word Families

As you learned in Chapters 1, 2, and 3, different word forms have different suffixes.

Ⓐ **Put each suffix in the box into the correct category in the chart.**

-al	-ance	-er	-ic	-ion
-ist	-ity	-ment	-tion	-try

Noun (person)	Noun (not a person)	Adjective

Ⓑ **Complete these sentences with the words in the box. All of the words are related to target words from the unit.**

complexity	involvement	relevance	technical	theorist

1. He got into trouble because of his _____ in criminal activity.

2. How is that point connected to what we are discussing? What is its _____ to the topic?

3. The _____ of that chemistry problem makes it very difficult to solve.

4. When you study computers, you must learn the _____ language that people who work with computers use.

5. She studies how different cultures are related, and then writes about her ideas. She is a cultural _____.

PLAYING WITH WORDS

Complete the puzzle with words you studied in Chapters 1–3.

Across

2. Talk to other people, work together with them, etc.

6. Something you say, write, do, or make that shows what you think or feel

10. Very, very bad

11. Facts, information, papers, etc., that prove that something is true

12. Connected in some way

13. Something that is difficult, especially in a way that is interesting

14. A quality that things, places, or people have that makes them attractive to look at

Down

1. The place where scientists or researchers do their work

3. Produced first (for example, a movie); not copied or based on anything else

4. The feeling that something is definitely true or definitely exists

5. Something important that someone says

7. To make a thin mark on a hard surface with something sharp or rough

8. According to what people say or report

9. Very fast

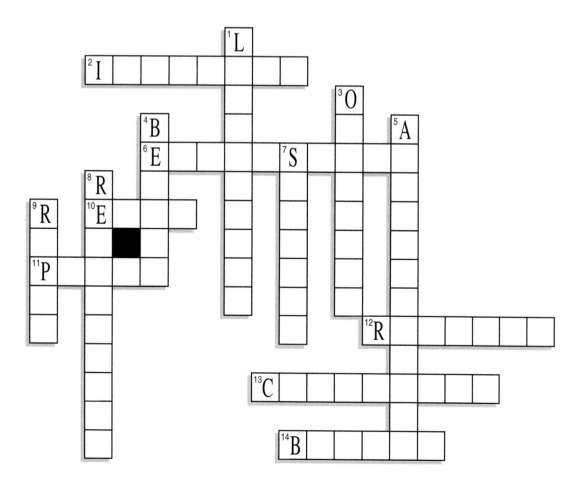

BUILDING DICTIONARY SKILLS

Finding Phrasal Verbs

Phrasal verbs do not have their own entries in most dictionaries. They are part of the entry for the verb. Usually, the phrasal verbs are listed at the end of all the definitions for the verb.

Look at the dictionary entry for phrasal verbs with *call*.

---

call[1] /kɔl/ *v*

1 ▸TELEPHONE◂ [I, T] to telephone someone: *I called about six o'clock but no one was home.* | *He said he'd call me tomorrow.* –see usage note at TELEPHONE . . .

. . . **9 call it a day** SPOKEN said when you want to stop working, either because you are tired or because you have done enough: *Come on, guys, let's call it a day.*

call back *phr v* [I,T **call** sb **back**] to telephone someone again, or to telephone someone who tried to telephone you earlier: *Okay, I'll call back around three.* | *Ms. Brinston is on another line; can she call you back later?*

call for sb/sth *phr v* [T] **1** to demand or need something in a particular situation: *Representatives are calling for an investigation into the scandal.* | *a situation that calls for immediate action* **2** to say that a particular type of weather is likely to happen: *The forecast calls for more rain.*

call in *phr v* **1** [T **call** sb ↔ **in**] to ask or order someone to come and help you with a difficult situation: *The governor called in the National Guard to deal with the riots.* **2** [I] to telephone the place where you work, especially to report something: *Jan called in sick this morning.* (=telephoned to say that she was too sick to come to work) **3** to telephone a radio or television show to give your opinion or ask a question

call sb/sth ↔ **off** *phr v* [T] **1** to decide that a planned event will not happen: *The game had to be called off due to bad weather.* **2** to order a dog or person to stop attacking someone: *Call off your dog!*

call on sb/sth *phr v* [T] **1** to formally ask someone to do something: *The UN has called on both sides to start peace talks.* **2** to visit someone for a short time: *a salesman calling on customers*

call out *phr v* **1** [I,T **call** sth ↔ **out**] to say something loudly: *"Hey!" she called out to him as he got into his car.* **2** [T **call** sb/sth ↔ **out**] to ask or order someone to come and help you with a difficult situation: *"Where's Dr. Cook?" "She's been called out."*

call up *phr v* **1** [I,T **call** sb ↔ **up**] to telephone someone: *Why don't you call Susie up and see if she wants to come?* **2** [T **call** sth ↔ **up**] to make information appear on a computer screen

---

Ⓐ **Look at the entry above. Circle the phrasal verbs and read the definitions. Complete the sentences with the correct particles. Be careful; you will not use all of the phrasal verbs listed.**

1. She called _____ to him in the crowd, but he didn't hear her.

2. Look how late it is! I'd better call my boss _____ and tell him I'll be late.

3. The baseball game was called _____ due to the rain.

4. The teacher always calls _____ me to answer the most challenging questions.

B Write your own sentences with the phrasal verbs from Exercise A.

1. _____

_____

2. _____

_____

3. _____

_____

4. _____

_____

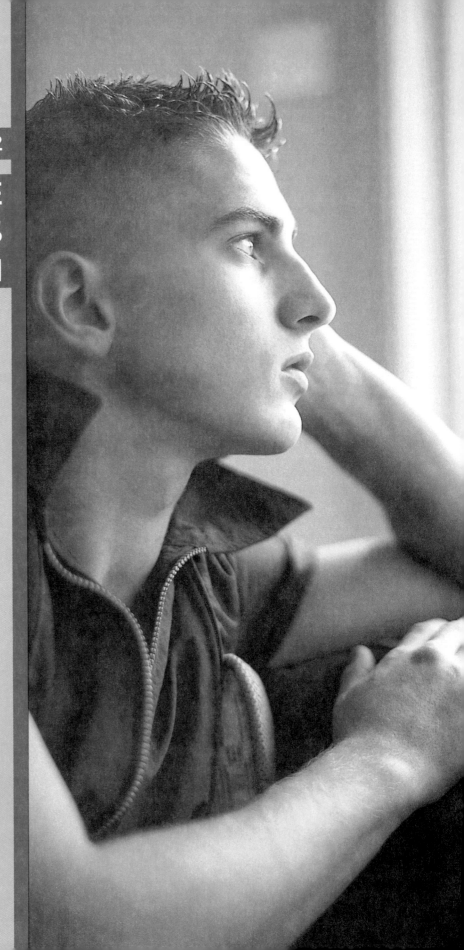

UNIT 2

THE CHALLENGES OF YOUTH

CHAPTER 4

Sleepy Teens

Why is this teenager so sleepy?

GETTING READY TO READ

 Complete the activity below. Then, talk with a partner or in a small group about the results.

Walk around the class, and ask your classmates about their sleeping habits. Try to find at least one person for each category. Write their names in the chart. Ask your classmates if they are happy with their sleep habits. If not, what would they like to change?

Gets enough sleep	Doesn't get enough sleep	Falls asleep during class	Sleeps less than 6 hours a night	Sleeps more than 8 hours a night	Likes to take naps	Usually goes to bed before 10:00

B The **boldfaced** words and phrases below appear in the reading. Which words are new to you? Circle them. Then, work with a partner. Read the definitions of the words, and complete the sentences next to each picture with the words.

experiment = a scientific test done to find out how something or someone will react in a particular situation, or to find out if a theory is true

patterns = regularly repeated arrangement of shapes, lines, or colors on a surface

in tears = crying

depressed = feeling very unhappy

1. The researchers in the sleep laboratory are doing an _____. They want to find out if teenagers' brains are active when they are sleeping.

2. They are checking the brain wave _____ of the people who are sleeping.

3. Like many other teenagers, this girl is _____. Sleep researchers think that it might be because she is not getting enough sleep.

4. This boy tried to go to bed at 8:30. He is _____ because he is upset that he can't fall asleep.

READING

Read the text once without stopping.

Sleepy Teens

1   When school superintendent[1] Russell Dever enters the local coffee shop at around 7:20 A.M., it is crowded with students. "The line is out the door because our high school kids are getting coffee," he said.

2   And they are not standing in line for the decaf[2]—they need the caffeine[3] to stay awake in class. Talk to American high school students and you hear the **complaints** about how late they **stay up**, how little they sleep—and how early they must be in class.

3   These days, there is increasing **concern** in schools across the United States about students who are not completely awake in morning classes. School **officials** in some states have even changed start times so teenagers can sleep later.

4   According to sleep **expert** Mary Carskadon, the fact that many teenagers work long hours outside of school and have computers and televisions in their bedrooms contributes to a serious **lack** of sleep. But, she said, the problem is also due to biology.[4] As the bodies of teenagers develop, their brains also change. These changes make teens more **likely** than adults to have trouble sleeping at night.

5   Teenagers need **at least** eight to nine hours of sleep a night, but the average teen gets a lot less. Carskadon's study, completed in the fall of 2001 with researcher Amy Wolfson, showed that nearly 30 percent of students in the tenth grade slept less than six hours on school nights. Less than 15 percent got more than eight hours of sleep each night. Eighth-graders averaged eight hours of sleep a night, although that age group, she said, needs at least nine hours a night.

6   Even more remarkable are the results of a 1997–1998 school year study. In that study, 12 out of 24 U.S. high school students who were part of an **experiment** at a sleep laboratory had brain wave **patterns** similar to those of someone with narcolepsy, a serious condition that affects sleep. "What's going on is that at 8:30 in the morning these kids . . . would

continued

---

[1] a *school superintendent* = someone who is responsible for all of the schools in a particular area of the United States

[2] *decaf* = short form of the phrase *decaffeinated coffee,* coffee that has had the caffeine removed

[3] *caffeine* = the chemical substance in coffee, tea, and some other drinks that makes people feel more active

[4] *biology* = the scientific study of living things

normally be in school sitting in a classroom, but . . . their brain is still in the middle of the night," said Carskadon.

7   Parent Dawn Dow says her 12-year-old son just cannot go to bed before 10 P.M. "Last year he was trying to put himself to bed at 8:30 and was coming in at 9:30 and 10 **in tears** saying, 'I just can't go to sleep.' It is not a case of children wanting to be up late . . . . It is a change in his chemistry."

8   So would letting teenagers wake up later make a difference? Kyla Wahlstrom of the University of Minnesota in the United States studies the effects of earlier school start times. She has looked at students in Edina and Minneapolis, two cities in Minnesota, where public school officials have moved high school starting times past 8:30 A.M. In Minneapolis, the middle school begins at 9:30 A.M. She said the later starting times have **reduced** student **absences**. They have also lowered **dropout** rates by 8 percent over four years. In addition, she said, teachers report that students are not sleeping at their desks during the first two hours of class anymore. She said 92 percent of parents from Edina reported that their teenagers are easier to live with. The students reported that they were feeling less **depressed** and were getting better grades.

9   Big changes in school start times may not be possible in some areas. However, Wahlstrom said her research shows that even small changes can contribute to a solution to this serious problem.

Notes

Mary Carskadon is professor of psychiatry[5] and human behavior at Brown University in Providence, Rhode Island, U.S.A. and director of sleep and chronobiology[6] at Bradley Hospital in East Providence, Rhode Island, U.S.A.

Amy Wolfson is a researcher at the College of the Holy Cross in Worcester, Massachusetts, U.S.A.

Kyla Wahlstrom is associate director[7] of the Center for Applied Research and Educational Improvement at the University of Minnesota, U.S.A.

---

[5] *psychiatry* = the study and treatment of mental illness
[6] *chronobiology* = the study of the effects of time on living things
[7] an *associate director* = someone who assists the director

Comprehension Check

Read these sentences. Circle T (true) or F (false). If you circle F, change the sentence to make it true. Check your answers with a classmate. If your answers are different, look back at the reading.

1. Often, teenagers sleep more than they should.   T   F

2. There are scientific reasons that explain why teenagers have difficulty sleeping at night.   T   F

3. The brains of teenagers are the same as the brains of adults.   T   F

4. Teenagers can do their best schoolwork in the early morning.   T   F

5. It's easier for adults to fall asleep at night than teenagers.   T   F

6. Some schools start their classes later so that teenage students can get more sleep in the morning.   T   F

EXPLORING VOCABULARY

Thinking about the Vocabulary

Guessing Strategy

Often, writers don't want to repeat a word, so they use a **synonym**. Synonyms are words that have similar meanings. If you don't know a word, look at the sentences nearby to see if there is a synonym. Look at the example.

> Some students who don't get enough sleep get **depressed**. And because they feel so unhappy, they can't concentrate on their schoolwork.

Based on the context, you can guess that the words *depressed* and *unhappy* are similar in meaning.

Try It!

Circle the word in the second sentence that is a synonym for the **boldfaced** target word.

> She said the later starting times have **reduced** student absences. They have also lowered dropout rates by 8 percent over four years.

Look at the target words and phrases. Which ones are new to you? Circle them here and in the reading. Then read "Sleepy Teens" again. Look at the context of each new word and phrase. Can you guess the meaning? Use the Guessing Strategy where possible.

Target Words and Phrases

complaints (2)	expert (4)	experiment (6)	absences (8)
stay up (2)	lack (4)	patterns (6)	dropout (8)
concern (3)	likely (4)	in tears (7)	depressed (8)
officials (3)	at least (5)	reduced (8)	

Using the Vocabulary

These sentences are **about the reading**. Complete them with the words and phrases in the box. Circle the words or phrases in the sentences that help you understand the meanings of the target words.

absences	at least	complaint	concern	dropout	experts
lack	likely	official	reduced	stay up	

1. Russell Dever is a school _____. He is responsible for several schools.

2. High school students _____ late at night, so they have trouble waking up early to go to school.

3. A common _____ from young people is that they don't get enough sleep. They are unhappy that school begins so early in the morning.

4. Some parents and school officials are worried that many high school students are too tired to learn. Because of their _____, some school officials have decided to change the time when high school classes start.

5. Researchers who study human sleep patterns say that teenagers get much less sleep than they really need. According to these _____, there are many different reasons for this serious _____ of sleep.

6. The main reason that teenagers are more _____ to have trouble sleeping than adults is due to the fact that their bodies are changing.

7. Most teenagers need _____ eight hours of sleep a night. In fact, it's even better if they get nine or ten hours.

8. When teenagers don't get enough sleep, they are more likely to miss class. In one school where start times were changed from 8:30 A.M. to 9:30 A.M., there are now fewer _____. The later start times seem to have _____ the number of students who don't go to class because they can't wake up in the morning.

9. The later start times have also lowered the _____ rate. This means that fewer students are quitting school.

DEVELOPING READING SKILLS

Understanding Main Ideas, Major Points, and Supporting Details

A reading generally has one **main idea**, with several **major points** to support it. Those major points are supported by **supporting details**. For example, in "Sleepy Teens" there is one main idea, three major points to support it, and many supporting details to illustrate the major points.

Answer these questions.

1. What is the main idea of "Sleepy Teens"?

   a. Some schools in the United States are experimenting with later school start times because experts say that teenagers will be happier and do better in school if they get more sleep.

   b. Many teenagers have difficulty falling asleep at night because of the biological changes in their brains and because they have televisions and computers in their rooms.

   c. Most American teenagers are depressed because they do not get enough sleep.

2. Which of these sentences are major points and which are supporting details? Write MP (major point) or SD (supporting detail).

   _MP_ **1.** There are many reasons that teenagers have trouble sleeping at night.

   _____ **2.** Research shows that many teenagers do not get enough sleep.

   _____ **3.** Many teenagers work long hours outside school.

   _____ **4.** Thirty percent of students in the tenth grade sleep less than six hours on school nights.

   _____ **5.** Schools that are experimenting with later start times are happy with the results.

_____ **6.** There are biological changes in the brains of teenagers that make it difficult for them to fall asleep at night.

_____ **7.** In one school that changed its start time from 8:30 to 9:30 A.M., the number of student absences has gone down.

_____ **8.** The students feel less depressed and get better grades when they get enough sleep.

EXPANDING VOCABULARY

Using the Vocabulary in New Contexts

These sentences use the target words and phrases in new contexts. Complete them with the words and phrases in the box.

absences	at least	complaint	concern	dropout	expert
lack	likely	official	reduce	stay up	

1. She has written more than ten books on education. She is an _____ on the subject.

2. I don't remember exactly how much money I have in the bank, but I know it's _____ $500. I might have more. I'll have to call the bank to check.

3. I'm going to take a nap so that I can _____ late to watch that TV special.

4. Take your umbrella. The weather report said that rain is _____ later this afternoon.

5. The service in that restaurant was terrible. I'm going to write a letter of _____ to the manager.

6. Thank you for your _____, but I'm fine. Don't worry about me.

7. If you want to lose weight, you must _____ the amount of food that you eat.

8. They are concerned about their son's complete _____ of interest in his studies. He doesn't seem to be interested in any subject.

9. You have too many _____. You need to make sure you attend all of the rest of the classes, or you will have to repeat the course.

10. My town has a serious _____ problem. Students are leaving high school early and can't find jobs.

11. He works for the government. He is the _____ who is responsible for public safety.

Word Families

Ⓐ Many words can be nouns, verbs, or adjectives. Look back at the reading. How are the target words below used? Write N (noun), V (verb), or A (adjective).

<u>N</u> absence   _____ complaint   _____ concern   _____ depressed

_____ dropout   _____ experiment   _____ official   _____ reduced

Ⓑ In the paragraph below, circle the words that are related to the target words from Exercise A. Then complete the chart with the words you circled.

It's 7:20 A.M., and teenagers are standing in line on the sidewalk in front of the local coffee shop. They complain that school starts too early in the morning, so they have to drink coffee to stay awake in class. They also complain of being depressed. Some students are absent because they can't wake up, and students who are absent a lot are more likely to drop out of school. This concerns many parents and school officials, so some schools are experimenting with a change in school start times. They hope that if teens can sleep a little later in the morning, they will be able to pay better attention in class. They also hope that the later start times will result in a reduction in the number of students who miss class. And some teens are reporting that their depression has disappeared since they started getting more sleep. If the experiment works, the schools will probably make the change official.

Noun	Verb	Adjective
	complain	

Studying Word Grammar

Some adjectives are formed by adding *-ing* or *-ed* to the end of a verb. These adjectives are called **participial adjectives**. Look at the examples.

Verb	Participial adjective (*-ing* form)	Participial adjective (*-ed* form)
Expresses an action	Describes a person or thing that **causes** a feeling or reaction.	Describes a person who **experiences** a feeling or reaction.
The story **depresses** John.	It is a **depressing** story.	John is **depressed** by the story.

A Complete the sentences with the *-ing* or *-ed* form of the **boldfaced** verbs.

1. Your theory **fascinates** me. I think it is _____.

2. Science **fascinates** my daughter. She is _____ by everything related to science.

3. That teacher likes to **challenge** her students. The homework she gives is usually _____.

4. I like my teachers to **challenge** me. I learn more when I feel _____.

5. If you **threaten** a wild animal, it might attack you. When wild animals feel _____, they often react with violence.

6. It is against the law to **threaten** someone with words or actions. I am going to report his _____ behavior to the police.

B Working with a partner, answer the questions. Make sure you use the correct form of the **boldfaced** words.

1. What is the most **fascinating** movie that you have ever seen? Explain why you felt so **fascinated** by it.
2. If a friend feels **depressed**, what can you do to make him or her feel better?
3. What is the most **challenging** thing that you have ever done?
4. Do you like easy classes, or do you prefer to feel **challenged**? Why?
5. What are some of the things people do when they feel **threatened**?

PUTTING IT ALL TOGETHER

Discussion

Share your ideas in a small group. As you talk, try to use the vocabulary below. Each time someone uses a target word or phrase, put a check (✓) next to it.

absence	at least	complaint
concern/concerned	depressed/depressing/depression	dropout/drop out
lack	likely	official
reduce/reduction	stay up	

1. Talk about problems that specifically affect teenagers. Give your opinion about the causes of the problems, and as a group come up with some possible solutions.

2. Not everyone agrees that changing school start times is such a good idea. As a group, come up with as many reasons as you can why schools should **not** change their start times.

Writing

Complete one or both of these writing topics. When you write, use at least five of the target words from the chapter. Underline the target words in your paper.

1. Imagine that you are the parent of a teenage girl in the Edina school system, and you do not agree with the change in the school start times. Write a letter about your concerns to an official at your daughter's high school.

2. Choose a problem that affects teenagers, and write an essay explaining the problems, the causes, and some possible solutions. Be sure to support your major points with details.

CHAPTER 5

Growing Up Gifted

Many chess prodigies start playing at a very young age.

GETTING READY TO READ

 Talk with a partner or in a small group.

1. Do you have a special skill or talent (for example in sports, music, painting, mathematics, science)? What is it? At what age did you become aware that you had talent?

2. If you could choose to be talented in one thing, what would you choose? Why?

3. A *child prodigy* is someone who shows remarkable talent in a particular subject at a very young age. Put a check (✓) next to the phrases that you believe would describe most child prodigies. Compare your answers, and discuss any differences.

_____ know a lot about many different things	_____ have a large vocabulary
_____ want to be perfect	_____ love school
_____ are happy	_____ are original thinkers
_____ are self-confident	

B The **boldfaced** words and phrases in the sentences below appear in the reading. Which words are new to you? Circle them. Then, work with a partner. Read the sentences about the reading, and choose the correct answers.

1. Pascal Charbonneau is an extremely talented chess player who has won many games. He is only a teenager, but he has already **achieved** more than most players twice his age. Someone who has *achieved* a lot has

   a. succeeded after trying hard.

   b. spent a lot of money.

   c. played very well.

2. In general, very talented young people like Pascal **tend to** enjoy learning about different things. Usually, they are interested in many subjects, not only the one in which they have talent. If you *tend to* do something, you

   a. take care of it.

   b. are involved in it.

   c. are likely to do it.

3. It is not easy to **survive** in the world of professional chess. Only the strongest players do well and earn enough money to live on. *Survive* means

   a. be successful enough to continue doing something.

   b. have fun and want to continue doing something.

   c. decide to stop doing something.

4. Although he is very talented at chess, Pascal doesn't feel different from his **peers**. He thinks that he's just an average teenager. Your *peers* are

   a. your parents.

   b. your teachers.

   c. other people your age.

READING

Read the text once without stopping.

Growing Up Gifted

1   Canadian teen chess[1] player Pascal Charbonneau has all the qualities of a child prodigy. He is smart, knows a lot about a variety of subjects, has **achieved** a lot at a young age, and is confident in his abilities. But Charbonneau does not like to be called a prodigy. "Winning a **championship** at this age is considered special, but I don't like thinking of myself as someone who is very different from other people," he said.

2   Like many 18-year-olds, Charbonneau is trying to decide where to go to college. School has always been easy for him, as it is for most **gifted** students. Many gifted students choose to finish school early to avoid getting bored, but Charbonneau decided to cruise through[2] his classes so he could **concentrate on** chess and some of his other interests, such as sports and French **literature**.

3   In general, gifted students **tend to** have an insatiable appetite[3] for information. They are also **perfectionists**. In addition, most are independent and **sensitive** to **injustice**. Other characteristics include specific ability in one area along with the ability to concentrate on it for a long time, excellent reading ability, a large vocabulary, originality, rapid mastery[4] of new skills, and an ability to see connections between ideas.

4   Having these characteristics can be challenging, even depressing, said Charbonneau. He is **critical** of even his best performances. "I'm rarely ever happy with what I do."

5   Charbonneau knows that the **pressure** on him will soon begin to grow, as every young chess player tries to become the next champion. That pressure has destroyed a lot of talented young people. For example, many young musical prodigies have walked away from their careers after discovering they will not become the star[5] of their dreams, says Francoys Gagne. Gagne is an expert on gifted children at the University of Quebec at Montreal, Canada. "When you are a prodigy, your goal is to become an international master musician," he said. "If you cannot become someone at

continued

---

[1] *chess* = a game for two players who move their playing pieces across a special board to try to get their opponent's King

[2] *cruise through* = do something well with very little effort

[3] *have an insatiable appetite* = want more and more of something

[4] *mastery* = complete understanding or great skill

[5] *a star* = a famous and successful performer in entertainment

the very top,[6] you are not interested in becoming a musician in an orchestra."[7]

6   World-famous violinist Itzhak Perlman has seen many talented young musicians simply **burn out**. "Rarely do you see people **survive**, and that's the goal, to survive your gift," he once told the *New York Times*.

7   Between 2 and 5 percent of young people are gifted, two to three years beyond their **peers**. But extremely gifted prodigies—the Beethovens and Mozarts—are much less common, perhaps one in a million, said Gagne. Here are some facts about several well-known child prodigies:

- Probably the most famous child prodigy of all, Wolfgang Amadeus Mozart (1756–1791) began writing music before he was five. By age six, he had written a remarkable amount of music and performed throughout Europe.

- Some of Ludwig van Beethoven's (1770–1827) music was **published** when he was only twelve. **Despite** losing his hearing as an adult, he continued to write music until his death.

- It is often said that the great scientist Albert Einstein (1879–1955) failed at school. In fact, he did well and could be described as a prodigy. Einstein was always a high achiever, although his best work was done when he was in his twenties.

----

[6] *at the very top* = successful and famous

[7] an *orchestra* = a large group of musicians playing many kinds of instruments

Comprehension Check

Read these sentences. Circle T (true), F (false), or ? (can't determine the answer from the reading). If you circle F, change the sentence to make it true. Check your answers with a classmate. If your answers are different, look back at the reading.

1. Pascal Charbonneau enjoys the attention he gets for being a child prodigy.   T   F   ?

2. Most child prodigies like to spend all of their time on just one subject.   T   F   ?

3. Gifted students often finish school earlier than their peers.   T   F   ?

4. Gifted children usually have the ability to study or practice one subject for a long time, until they become almost perfect at it.   T   F   ?

5. Most gifted children have parents who put a lot of pressure on them to succeed.   T   F   ?

6. Most musical prodigies become famous musicians.   T   F   ?

EXPLORING VOCABULARY

Thinking about the Vocabulary

Guessing Strategy

You learned in Chapter 2 that one way to guess the meaning of an adjective is to determine whether it has a positive or negative meaning. In fact, the same strategy can be used with any part of speech—adjective, noun, verb, or adverb. Look at the example.

> He's smart, has **achieved** a lot at a young age, and is confident in his abilities.

Because the words *smart* and *confident* have positive meanings, you should be able to guess that the verb *achieve* has a positive meaning too.

Try It!

Find these target words or phrases in the reading. Do they have a positive or a negative meaning? Write **P** (positive) or **N** (negative).

burn out _____   championship _____   critical _____

Look at the target words and phrases. Which ones are new to you? Circle them here and in the reading. Then read "Growing Up Gifted" again. Look at the context of each new word and phrase. Can you guess the meaning? Use the Guessing Strategy where possible.

Target Words and Phrases

achieved (1)	literature (2)	injustice (3)	survive (6)
championship (1)	tend to (3)	critical (4)	peers (7)
gifted (2)	perfectionists (3)	pressure (5)	published (7)
concentrate on (2)	sensitive (3)	burn out (6)	despite (7)

Using the Vocabulary

These sentences are **about the reading**. Complete them with the words and phrases in the box. Circle the words or phrases in the sentences that help you understand the meanings of the target words.

burn out	championships	concentrate on	critical
despite	gifted	injustice	literature
published	perfectionists	pressure	sensitive

1. _____ children have special talents, and usually learn things at an earlier age than their peers.

2. Gifted children can usually _____ one subject for a long period of time, without getting bored.

3. Most gifted children are interested in many different subjects. For example, Pascal Charbonneau has won many chess _____, but he also likes to read French _____ and play sports.

4. Another characteristic of gifted children is that they understand other people; they are _____ to the feelings of others.

5. Gifted children do not like it when other people are treated unfairly. They do not like to see _____.

6. Prodigies are rarely satisfied with their performance. They are _____ of themselves, even when they perform brilliantly.

7. Prodigies don't like to make even a very small mistake. They are _____.

8. The life of a musical prodigy is not easy. Everyone expects them to perform brilliantly all of the time. Some prodigies cannot deal with the constant _____ and decide to quit performing.

9. Because of the pressure on them, many gifted young musicians get so tired that they stop performing. They _____.

10. Beethoven was one of the most famous musical prodigies. He wrote and _____ music at a very young age.

11. _____ their talent, many prodigies never become famous.

DEVELOPING READING SKILLS

Understanding Major Points

Answer these questions in your own words. Do not copy from the reading.

1. Why might it be depressing to be gifted?

   _____

   _____

2. Why don't many young musical prodigies end up having a career in music?

   _____

   _____

3. The reading says that one of the characteristics of gifted children is a tendency to be sensitive to injustice. The reading does not say why this is true, but we can imagine the reasons. Why do you think gifted children might be more sensitive to injustice than other people?

   _____

   _____

Understanding Supporting Details

Answer these questions.

1. In order to be considered gifted, how much more advanced than their peers do children have to be?

   _____

   _____

2. What percentage of the general population is gifted?

   _____

   _____

Understanding Inference

An **inference** is more than just a guess. You should always have a good reason for making an inference, and you should be careful that your inference does not go too far beyond what is written in the text. Look at the sentence.

> Einstein was always a high achiever, although his best work was done when he was in his 20s.

It would *not* be correct to infer from this sentence that Einstein did good work **only** when he was in his 20s. That inference goes too far beyond what is written.

Read these sentences from "Growing Up Gifted." Then, read the two sentences that follow. Put a check (✓) next to the sentence in each set that is a reasonable inference based on the sentences from the reading. The numbers in parentheses are the paragraphs that the sentences come from.

1. Having these characteristics can be challenging, even depressing, said Charbonneau. He is critical of even his best performances. "I'm rarely ever happy with what I do." (4)

   —— Many child prodigies are unhappy when they perform poorly.

   —— Child prodigies are often unhappy because they always want to be perfect.

2. Many young musical prodigies have walked away from their careers after discovering they won't become the star of their dreams, says Francoys Gagne. (5)

   —— Francoys Gagne believes that musical prodigies should continue their careers in music, even if they can't become stars.

   —— According to Francoys Gagne, many young musical prodigies are not happy having just an ordinary career as a musician.

3. World-famous violinist Itzhak Perlman has seen many talented young musicians simply burn out. "Rarely do you see people survive, and that's the goal, to survive your gift," he once told the *New York Times.* (6)

   —— Many gifted young musicians do not have successful careers, despite having remarkable talent.

   —— Many young musicians are not quite talented enough to achieve their goals.

EXPANDING VOCABULARY

Using the Vocabulary in New Contexts

These sentences use the target words and phrases in new contexts. Complete them with the words and phrases in the box.

burn out	championship	concentrate on	critical
despite	gifted	injustice	literature
perfectionist	pressure	published	sensitive

1. He is the oldest player to ever win an international tennis _____.

2. I'm concerned that you are working too hard. I know you enjoy your job now, but if you aren't careful, you'll _____ by the time you're 30!

3. She's a gifted mystery writer. She's already written at least three books. Her first book was _____ ten years ago.

4. Be careful how you talk to him. He's very _____. Yesterday, he was in tears because of something one of the other kids said to him.

5. I hate it when teachers treat their male and female students differently. The _____ really makes me angry.

6. _____ the complete lack of proof that he was involved in the crime, he was arrested and put in jail.

7. In English _____, William Shakespeare stands out as one of the most brilliant writers.

8. I'm a _____. I am never satisfied unless I do something exactly right.

9. Stop playing around on the computer and _____ your homework! It's almost time for bed.

10. After 100 performances in just three months, she got very sick and had to go in the hospital. The doctors said that the _____ of performing live seven nights a week was too much for her.

11. My daughter has been placed in a program for _____ children. Her teachers think that the challenge of interacting with other talented children will be good for her.

12. He's very sensitive. He doesn't like it when his teachers are even just a little _____ of his work.

Word Families

When you learn a new word, you can build your vocabulary by learning forms of the words that are in the same family. Sometimes within the same word family, there is more than one word for a word form. Usually, the two words have related, but different, meanings. Look at these sentences.

You shouldn't **criticize** him. He is doing the best he can.
Would you please read my essay and **critique** it?

The verbs *criticize* and *critique* are in the same word family. They have related, but different, meanings. *Criticize* means "to judge someone or something severely." *Critique* means "to judge whether someone or something is good or bad."

Study the chart. Then, complete the sentences with words from the chart. If there are two words listed for one word form, look up the words in the dictionary. Be careful; you will not use all the words.

Noun (person)	Noun (thing)	Verb	Adjective
	achievement	achieve	
	concentration	concentrate	
critic	criticism, critique	criticize, critique	critical
publisher	publication	publish, publicize	
	tendency	tend	
	pressure	pressure, pressurize	
perfectionist	perfection	perfect	perfect
champion	championship		

1. He received an award for remarkable _____ in the arts.

2. Just like her mother, she has a _____ to get depressed.

3. He is a _____ of rare books.

4. There was a party to celebrate the _____ of his most recent book.

5. The new theory is fascinating, but experts are likely to _____ the way the researchers did their experiments.

6. I'm tired of all the complaints and _____. I'm just trying to do the best job I can.

7. Thank you for your _____ of my performance in the competition. It was very helpful to me.

8. Please watch my performance and _____ it. Don't be afraid to be honest!

9. I did badly on the test because my _____ was poor.

10. Please don't _____ him. You know how sensitive he is.

11. He beat all of his competitors. He is the new _____.

12. He's a good soccer player, but he wants to be better. He wants to _____ his skills.

13. The film _____ didn't like the movie at all, but I loved it.

14. It doesn't matter how hard you try. You will never achieve

   _____.

15. His test score was _____. He got every answer right.

Studying Word Grammar

Prepositions can be followed by nouns or pronouns. Since **gerunds** (base form of verb + *-ing*) act as nouns, they can follow prepositions too. Look at the sentence from the reading.

   "If you cannot become someone at the very top, you are not interested **in becoming** a musician in an orchestra."

A Complete the sentences with the *-ing* form of the verbs below.

   achieve   **burn out**   **criticize**   **pressure**   **publish**

1. Great news! There are two companies interested in _____ your new book. You're going to have a career as a writer!

2. He's decided to take a long vacation. He's been working so hard lately that he's afraid of _____.

3. Instead of _____ everyone else's work, why don't you concentrate on improving your own?

4. I don't believe in _____ children to do things that they aren't ready for. If we push them too much when they are young, they'll burn out.

5. Despite _____ more than anyone else in his class, he was not selected to participate in the end-of-year performance.

B Complete the sentences with information about yourself. Use a gerund after the preposition.

1. I like to be left alone when I'm concentrating on _____.

2. I don't believe in _____.

3. Instead of _____, I _____.

4. Despite _____, I _____.

PUTTING IT ALL TOGETHER

Discussion

Share your ideas in a small group. As you talk, try to use the vocabulary below. Each time someone uses a target word or phrase, put a check (✓) next to it.

achieve/achievement	burn out	champion/championship
concentrate on	critic/critical/criticize/criticism	gifted
just/unjust	peer	perfectionist/perfect/perfection
pressure	sensitive	survive
tend to		

1. Sometimes, school officials take the best students out of regular classes and put them into classes with other gifted children. Make a list of the advantages and disadvantages of separating the gifted students from the other students. Consider how this might affect not only the gifted students but also the other students.

2. When you were a child, did your parents ever pressure you to develop a talent or skill, or to achieve something difficult? If so, explain what happened. Was it a positive or a negative experience? If you have children, will you pressure them in the same way? Why or why not?

Writing

Complete one or both of these writing topics. When you write, use at least five of the target words from the chapter. Underline the target words in your paper.

1. Write an essay in support of or against separating gifted and other students into different classes.

2. Choose a famous person who was a child prodigy. Do some research either at the library or on the Internet. Then, write an essay about the person. Your essay should include the following information:

   • Date and place of birth

   • Age that the prodigy's talent was discovered

   • How the prodigy's talent was discovered

   • Major achievements

   • Current situation (for someone who is still living)

   • Any other interesting information that you discover

CHAPTER 6

School Bullies

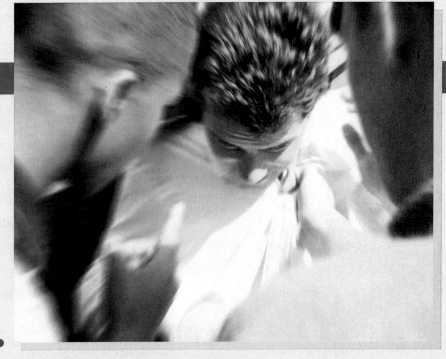

Bullying: What can be done?

GETTING READY TO READ

 Talk with a partner or in a small group.

1. A **bully** is someone who uses his or her strength or power to frighten or hurt someone who is weaker. A **victim** is someone who has been attacked or treated very badly. Were there any bullies in your school? Describe them for your group. What did they look like? Who were their victims? What did they do to their victims?

2. Put a check (✓) next to the words that you think describe most bullies. Compare your answers with those of your group members.

   _____ popular   _____ confident   _____ given a lot of freedom by parents

   _____ male   _____ female   _____ depressed

   _____ sensitive _____ competitive

3. Put a check (✓)next to the words that you think describe most victims of bullies. Compare your answers to those of your group members.

   _____ thin   _____ confident   _____ intelligent   _____ depressed

   _____ sensitive _____ male   _____ female   _____ from poor families

B The **boldfaced** words in the paragraph below appear in the reading. Which words are new to you? Circle them. Then, work with a partner. Read this paragraph introducing the topic of the reading, and match the words with their definitions.

Go into any school, and you will probably find at least one school bully. The school bully usually chooses a weaker classmate as a victim. Bullies **pick on** their victims in many different ways. Their **aggression** involves words, actions, or both. Some bullies use just words to frighten their victims, but others also attack their victims **physically**. Most victims do not **stand up for** themselves, even when they are attacked repeatedly.

Word	Definition
_____ **1.** pick on	**a.** defend
_____ **2.** aggression	**b.** treat someone in a way that is not kind
_____ **3.** physically	**c.** angry or threatening behavior or feelings that often result in fighting
_____ **4.** stand up for	**d.** by using the body rather than the mind or feelings

READING

Read the text once without stopping.

School Bullies[1]

1   A middle school student is regularly beaten and threatened by his classmates. A 14-year-old boy dies after being pushed down the school stairs by a classmate. Parents send their three-year-old children to special classes in self-defense so that they will not become **victims** when they begin school. These shocking stories are all real examples of an ugly side of school life: bullying.

2   Dan Olweus, a professor of psychology[2] at Bergen University in Norway, has spent 20 years studying **aggression** in schools. Dr. Olweus **examined** the results of a **survey** of 150,000 Norwegian[3] students. The

continued

---

[1] a *bully* = someone who uses their strength or power to frighten or hurt someone who is weaker

[2] *psychology* = the study of the mind and how it works

[3] *Norwegian* = coming from Norway

data showed that 15 percent were either bullies or victims. His research is interesting because it challenges what people tend to believe about bullying.

3   First, bullies do not always **pick on** the **overweight** kid wearing glasses. Second, bullies are often popular, and they do not become bullies due to low **self-esteem**. Third, the size of the school, class size, and the **economic** and social **background** of the students do not make much difference in the amount of bullying. Fourth, bullying does not tend to take place as students are going to and from school. Fifth, bullying is not related to competition among students. Finally, more boys than girls are involved in bullying, and many girls are bullied by boys.

4   What do the victims of bullying have in common? Dr. Olweus's research shows that "the typical victim tends to be more **anxious** and less secure than his classmates and usually has a negative **attitude** towards violence."

5   In surveys, parents of male victims report that the boys were cautious[4] and sensitive at an early age. They probably had difficulty **standing up for** themselves, and therefore were disliked by their peers. These characteristics, combined with the fact that many of the boys were **physically** weak, contributed to their becoming victims of bullying.

6   The typical bully, on the other hand, is neither anxious nor insecure, and has a strong need for power and dominance.[5] "Too little love and care in childhood and too much **freedom** are conditions that strongly contribute to the development of bullies," says Dr. Olweus. In other studies that he has **conducted**, Dr. Olweus has found that about 60 percent of boys who were bullies between the ages of 11 and 15 had been involved in criminal activity by the time they were 24. Dr. Olweus's research has also shown that bullying victims are much more likely to be depressed than children who have not been bullied.

7   **On the basis of** his research, Dr. Olweus has designed a program that has reduced bullying by 50 percent in 42 Norwegian schools. It is now used by schools all over the world. The program, which is described in Olweus's book, *Bullying at School—What We Know and What We Can Do* (Oxford: Blackwell Publishing, 1993.), starts with an anonymous questionnaire.[6] Next, there is a school conference day to discuss the answers to the questionnaire. Then there are meetings with both parents and teachers involved.

continued

---

[4] *cautious* = careful to stay away from danger or risks

[5] *dominance* = the fact of being more powerful, more important, or more noticeable than other people

[6] an *anonymous questionnaire* = a written set of questions given to a large number of people who answer without giving their names

8   At school, teachers and other adults pay close attention to children's behavior. Adults are always present—not only during class time, but also between classes and at lunch. In class, students and their teachers write rules against bullying and have regular meetings to discuss the subject. Immediate action is taken if anyone thinks that a child is being bullied, and victims are protected. Bullies and victims are spoken to separately. In serious cases, school officials **contact** the parents.

9   Dr. Olweus strongly believes that bullies can be beaten. However, schools must take responsibility for developing programs like his to deal with this serious problem.

Comprehension Check

Read these sentences. Circle T (true) or F (false). If you circle F, change the sentence to make it true. Check your answers with a classmate. If your answers are different, look back at the reading.

1. Dr. Olweus's research explains the causes of bullying and ways to deal with the problem.   T   F

2. Bullies do not have many friends.   T   F

3. Bullies do not have a lot of self-esteem.   T   F

4. Victims of bullying usually do not like violence and do not fight back against bullies.   T   F

5. Most bullies did not get enough love when they were children.   T   F

6. According to Dr. Olweus, it is the responsibility of parents, not schools, to deal with the problem of bullying.   T   F

EXPLORING VOCABULARY

Thinking about the Vocabulary

Guessing Strategy

By thinking about the logical relationship between the subject and the object of a verb, you can often guess the meaning of the verb. Look at the example.

Bullies often **pick on** children who are smaller and weaker than they are.

The object of the target phrasal verb *pick on* is *children who are smaller and weaker than they are*. The subject is *bullies*. Bullies often treat smaller, weaker children badly.

Try It!

Read the sentences, and write a definition of the **boldfaced** target word.

> Dr. Olweus **examined** the results of a study of 150,000 students. He learned that 15 percent of the students were either victims or bullies.

Examine means _____

Look at the target words and phrases. Which ones are new to you? Circle them here and in the reading. Then read "School Bullies" again. Look at the context of each new word and phrase. Can you guess the meaning? Use the Guessing Strategy where possible.

Target Words and Phrases

victims (1)	pick on (3)	anxious (4)	freedom (6)
aggression (2)	overweight (3)	attitude (4)	conducted (6)
examined (2)	self-esteem (3)	standing up for (5)	on the basis of (7)
survey (2)	economic (3)	physically (5)	contact (8)
data (2)	background (3)		

Using the Vocabulary

These sentences are **about the reading**. Complete them with the words and phrases in the box. Circle the words or phrases in the sentences that help you understand the meanings of the target words.

anxious	attitude	background	conducted	contact
data	economic	examines	freedom	on the basis of
overweight	self-esteem	survey		

1. Dr. Olweus has led many studies on the causes of bullying. He has _____ a lot of research on the topic.

2. For more than 20 years, Dr. Olweus has been collecting information from bullies and victims. He then _____ that information to find patterns to explain why some students become bullies, while others become victims.

3. Dr. Olweus has collected information about bullies from countries all over the world. He then studies the _____ to understand school aggression.

4. In one large study of 150,000 students in Norway, 15 percent of the students who answered a _____ on bullying reported that they were either victims or bullies.

5. Bullying happens in both rich and poor schools. The _____ situation of the school's town has no effect on the amount of bullying.

6. The economic and social _____ of a bully are often exactly the same as that of his victim.

7. Physically weak children are often victims of bullies. However, _____ children are not any more likely to be picked on than thin children.

8. Victims have a tendency to worry a lot. They are often very _____.

9. Bullies are often very self-confident. They have high _____.

10. Typically, victims do not like violence. Their _____, or feeling, toward it is negative.

11. Bullies' parents do not pay enough attention to their children when they are small. Often, their children have the _____ to do whatever they want to do.

12. In schools that follow Dr. Olweus's program, school officials _____ both sets of parents when their children are involved in bullying. They ask them to come into school to talk about the problem.

13. Dr. Olweus's program is so effective because it is the result of years of careful research. He designed the program _____ research.

DEVELOPING READING SKILLS

Understanding Main Ideas

Answer this question.

What is "School Bullies" about? Write one or two sentences that give the main idea.

_____

_____

_____

Understanding Inference

A **misconception** is an idea that is wrong or untrue but that people believe because they do not understand it correctly. If you can identify the misconception in a text, you can use inference to figure out the truth about the idea.

Read paragraph 3 on page 68 again and label the following statements T (for true) or M (for misconception).

__M__ 1. Most victims are overweight and wear glasses.

_____ 2. Bullies are popular with their peers.

_____ 3. Bullies are insecure.

_____ 4. There is more bullying in big schools with large classes than in small schools with small classes.

_____ 5. The amount of bullying in rich schools is about the same as the amount of bullying in poorer schools.

_____ 6. Most bullying happens when students are arriving at or leaving school.

_____ 7. Bullying often starts when students are competing against each other.

_____ 8. Boys do not usually bully girls.

EXPANDING VOCABULARY

Using the Vocabulary in New Contexts

These sentences use the target words and phrases in new contexts. Complete them with the words and phrases in the box.

anxious	attitude	background	conduct	contact
data	economic	examine	freedom	on the basis of
overweight	self-esteem	survey		

1. My daughter really doesn't like to read. Her _____ towards her literature class is terrible.

2. When we finish the experiment, we will _____ the results and then write up a report.

3. I believe in _____ and justice for all people.

4. Tim and Mark are brothers, but they don't look at all alike. Tim is tall and thin, while Mark is short and a little bit _____.

5. My husband lost his job _____ just one customer complaint. I think that is very unjust.

6. Despite the town's serious _____ problems, the people voted to buy new computers for the schools.

7. I can't concentrate on my work because I'm so _____ about my math test.

8. We don't have enough _____ on the causes of depression. We need to conduct more research.

9. The school is trying to find out why there are so many absences among students in the third grade. They have asked the parents of all third graders to complete a _____.

10. People with a strong educational _____ often have a higher social position than people with less education.

11. If you have any questions, _____ our office immediately.

12. My son never thinks he does anything right. His teachers say that he doesn't have much _____.

13. In order to test their theories, scientists often _____ experiments.

Word Families

 A Complete the chart with the correct forms of the words. Check your answers in your dictionary. There may be more than one word for some word forms.

Noun (thing)	Verb	Adjective
aggression		
		anxious
		economic
	examine	
survey		
freedom		

B Working with a partner, answer the questions. Make sure you use the correct forms of the **boldfaced** words.

1. What will you do if your child is **aggressive**?
2. What kinds of health problems can **anxiety** cause?
3. How is the **economy** of your country?
4. If you had to **economize,** what things would you stop spending money on?
5. How often do you go to the doctor for a physical **examination**?
6. If researchers want to find out about bullies, whom should they **survey**?
7. Do you think that scientists who use animals in research should **free** the animals when they finish using them in experiments? Why or why not?
8. When is your next English **exam**?

Studying Collocations

Certain nouns are used with certain verbs. Look at the sentence.

Dr. Olweus **conducted a survey on** school bullies.

The noun *survey* is often used with the verb *conduct*. Other nouns that are often used with *conduct* are *research* and *experiment*. When *conduct* is used with these nouns, it means "do," and it follows this pattern:

Conduct (= do)	a survey research an experiment	on	object (what or who the survey, experiment, or research is about)

Working with a partner, answer the questions. Make sure you use the correct form of the boldfaced words.

1. Do you think that it's morally wrong for scientists to **conduct experiments on** laboratory animals? Why or why not?

2. If you could **conduct a survey on** the lives of gifted children, what questions would you ask?

3. What are some of the things that doctors and scientists are **conducting research on** today?

PUTTING IT ALL TOGETHER

Discussion

Work in a small group.

Design a survey with at least five questions, and use at least five target words from this chapter. When you have finished writing your survey, have your teacher check it. Then, conduct the survey on the other members of your class, or peers from other classes. Finally, present your results to the class in a group presentation.

Choose one of the following survey topics:

      School bullies   **Teenagers**   **Special talents**

Writing

Complete one or both of these writing topics. When you write, use at least five of the target words from the chapter. Underline the target words in your paper.

1. Write a report on your group survey project. Your report should include
   - The topic
   - What you were trying to find out
   - Who participated
   - How many people participated
   - The results
   - Interesting patterns in the results
   - What you think about the results

2. Write a story about a school bully. It can be a true story, or you can use your imagination. Try to make the story "come alive" for your reader. Tell the story from one of the following points of view:

- The bully
- The bully's friend
- The bully's parents
- The victim
- The victim's friend
- The victim's parents
- A teacher

Wrap-up

REVIEWING READING SKILLS AND VOCABULARY

Read the text. Do not use a dictionary.

1   After conducting much research, scientists now have definite proof of what parents have known for centuries: teenagers are different from everyone else. And the differences go much deeper than simple behavior. In fact, the brains of teenagers are very different from those of children or adults.

2   Until recently, scientists believed that the human brain was fully developed by the age of three. According to this theory, the teen behaviors that most concern parents—risk-taking, a lack of sensitivity to how their actions affect both themselves and others, increased aggression, reduced concentration, a negative attitude—were thought to be due to bad parenting or changes in body chemistry. However, new technology has allowed researchers to examine the healthy brain at work, and what they have discovered might surprise you. Not only does the brain continue to grow past the age of three, but the brain of a teenager is larger than that of an adult.

3   As teen brains are flooded with chemicals during adolescence,[1] the brain grows. However, at the same time, the cells of the brain that are used more compete with those that are used less. Only the cells[2] and the connections between the cells that are used the most will survive the competition. Those that are used less begin to die off until the brain reaches what will be its adult size.

4   The way that teens spend their time influences which connections remain, and which disappear. On the basis of this knowledge, experts advise parents to be sensitive to how their teenagers spend their time. What teens do today will affect their brains for the rest of their lives.

---

[1] *adolescence* = the period of time, from about 13 to 17 years of age, when a young person is developing into an adult

[2] a *cell* = the smallest part of an animal or plant that can exist on its own

Comprehension Check

Read these sentences. Circle T (true), F (false), or ? (can't determine the answer from the reading). If you circle F, change the sentence to make it true.

1. Scientists now know that the human brain continues to develop for years after we are born.   T   F   ?

2. The brain of a three-year-old is larger than the brain of a teenager.   T   F   ?

3. People with big brains are smarter than people with smaller brains.   T   F   ?

4. If a teenager uses a particular part of the brain too much, the brain cells in that area will die off.   T   F   ?

5. Teen behavior has an important effect on the physical development of the brain.   T   F   ?

Guessing Meaning from Context

Answer this question.

What is the meaning of *flooded with* in the first line of paragraph 3?

_____

Understanding Main Ideas

Answer this question.

What is the main idea of the reading?

_____

_____

Understanding Inference

Read these sentences from the text. Then, read the two sentences that follow. Put a check (✓) next to the sentence in each set that is a reasonable inference based on the sentences from the reading. The numbers in parentheses are the paragraphs that the sentences come from.

1. Scientists now have definite proof of what parents have known for centuries: teenagers are different from everyone else. (1)

   _____ Until recently, scientists did not know exactly why teenagers behave the way that they do.

   _____ A long time ago, parents proved that teenagers are different from everyone else.

2. According to this theory, the teen behaviors that most concern parents—risk-taking, a lack of sensitivity to how their actions affect both themselves and others, increased aggression, reduced concentration, a negative attitude—were thought to be due to bad parenting or changes in body chemistry. (2)

_____ Experts do not believe anymore that the behavior of parents or changes in body chemistry are the causes of negative teenage behavior.

_____ Parents used to think that their teenagers were bad because they took risks, were aggressive, and had negative attitudes.

3. On the basis of this knowledge, experts advise parents to be sensitive to how their teenagers spend their time. What teens do today will affect their brains for the rest of their lives. (4)

_____ Experts think that if parents are more sensitive to what teenagers need, teenagers will behave better.

_____ Experts think that parents should help their teenagers to develop healthy patterns of behavior.

EXPANDING VOCABULARY

Studying Word Grammar

Some words are actually a combination of two words. They are called **compound words**. *Dropout* is an example of a compound word. Some compound words have a special type of punctuation called a *hyphen* (-) that combines the two words together into one word. *Self-esteem* is an example of a compound word containing a hyphen.

Read the following sentences, and write definitions of the boldfaced words.

1. She is an excellent student, but she is never satisfied with her grades. She is an **overachiever**.

   Overachievers are people who _put a lot of pressure on themselves to_ _perform well, and are very unhappy if they don't achieve everything_ _they want to._

2. He's very clever, but he is lazy. He could be successful if he tried a little harder. He is an **underachiever**.

   Underachievers are people who _____

3. Artists try to communicate their ideas and feelings through their art. **Self-expression** is very important to them.

   Self-expression is _____

Studying Phrasal Verbs

Some phrasal verbs are followed by a direct object (a person or thing). Other phrasal verbs have no object. For example, the phrasal verb *stand up for* must have an object, but the phrasal verb *stand out* never takes an object.

A Read these sentences, and pay attention to whether the **boldfaced** phrasal verb takes an object or doesn't take an object. Write O (object) or NO (no object).

1. _____ He went to college, but he **dropped out** after just one year.

2. _____ Stop **picking on** your little brother.

3. _____ How late did you **stay up** last night?

B Write answers to these questions. Use the **boldfaced** phrasal verbs in your answers.

1. What are some of the reasons that teenagers **drop out** of high school?

   _____

   _____

   _____

2. Has anyone ever **picked on** you? Who?

   _____

   _____

   _____

3. How late do you usually **stay up**?

   _____

   _____

   _____

Word Families

The suffix *-ize* shows that a word is a verb. Here are some verbs that end in *-ize*. (The words in parentheses are target words from the unit that are in the same word family.)

criticize (critical)   economize (economic)   pressurize (pressure)

publicize (publish)   victimize (victim)

Complete these sentences with the verbs on the bottom of page 80.

1. Don't let that bully _____ you! Protect yourself!

2. My husband lost his job, so we really have to _____.

3. I don't like to _____ my problems. I prefer to keep them private.

4. You shouldn't _____ your teacher. She is only trying to help you.

5. Before engineers figured out how to _____ the inside of airplanes, flying at very high altitudes was not possible.

PLAYING WITH WORDS

There are 12 target words from Unit 2 in this puzzle. The words go across (→) and down (↓). Find the words and circle them. Then use them to complete the sentences on the next page.

```
R  E  B  A  C  K  G  R  O  U  N  D  S  A
D  M  P  O  R  D  E  S  P  I  T  E  M  A
Q  W  E  T  L  I  O  L  J  P  O  N  R  B
U  C  R  E  P  A  T  T  E  R  N  D  O  S
G  I  F  K  Z  H  V  C  D  K  S  Q  T  E
J  F  E  A  G  G  R  E  S  S  I  O  N  N
G  H  C  O  T  S  B  F  R  P  J  R  I  C
I  V  T  F  S  U  R  V  I  V  E  B  Y  E
F  L  I  F  C  E  L  T  R  O  P  L  E  S
T  W  O  I  M  D  I  N  V  H  A  A  D  N
E  G  N  C  C  U  K  Y  L  Z  F  C  A  U
D  B  I  I  N  L  E  W  X  P  J  K  T  W
A  X  S  A  O  Y  L  T  A  G  L  I  A  O
F  M  T  L  X  S  Y  A  M  B  A  L  L  Y
```

1. He was a high-school dropout. He does not have a strong educational

    _____.

2. The researcher's _____ prove that his theory is correct.

3. Children whose parents are depressed are more _____ to become depressed themselves.

4. Some people think that the rise in physical _____ in the schools is due to the violence that children see on television.

5. Why do you have so many _____? Have you been sick?

6. She's a _____. She always wants to do everything exactly right. She hates making mistakes.

7. He did poorly on the test due to his _____ of knowledge.

8. If you don't study, you will never _____ at that university.

9. I would like to find curtains that match the _____ on the sofa.

10. He is a government _____, so he cannot be too critical of the government.

11. They went to the beach _____ the bad weather.

12. She has won several piano competitions. She is very _____.

BUILDING DICTIONARY SKILLS

Finding the Correct Meaning

Many words have more than one meaning. Look at the dictionary entries below. Read each sentence and write the number of the meaning.

> **sur·vive** /sɚˈvaɪv/ v [I,T] **1** to continue to live after an accident, illness, etc.: *Only one person survived the crash.* **2** to continue to exist or be involved in an activity in spite of difficulties: *Few small businesses survived the recession.* | *The surviving teams will play each other on Sunday.*

1. a. _____ Only three people **survived** the airplane crash.

    b. _____ It isn't easy to **survive** in the business world.

pres·sure[1] /ˈprɛʃɚ/ *n* **1** [U] an attempt to make someone do something by using influence, arguments, threats etc.: *The group is **putting pressure** on the state to change the smoking laws.* | *NASA was **under** political **pressure** to start a new space program.* **2** [C,U] the conditions of your work, family, or way of living that make you anxious and cause problems: *Their team always plays best **under pressure**.* | *the pressures of modern life* **3** [C,U] the force or weight that is being put on something, or the strength of this force or weight: *The pressure of the water turns the wheel.* | *The gas is stored at **high/low pressure**.*

2. a. _____ She's having a hard time. The **pressure** of work, school, and family are too much for her.

b. _____ There is a lot of **pressure** on him to accept the job.

c. _____ Did you check the tire **pressure**? Do we need to add air?

back·ground /ˈbækɡraʊnd/ *n* **1** the type of education, experiences, and family that someone has: *The kids have very different religious backgrounds* **2** the sounds, things, movements etc. that are in or happening in a place or picture but that are not the main thing you see or hear: *I could hear cars honking **in the background**.* **3** [singular, U] ⇨ BACKDROP

3. a. _____ We didn't give her the job because she doesn't have the educational **background** we are looking for.

b. _____ When I was talking to my friend on the phone, I could hear her son crying in the **background**.

GENETICS: THE SCIENCE OF WHO WE ARE

CHAPTER 7

The Science of Genetics

Gregor Mendel and his pea plant experiment

GETTING READY TO READ

 Talk with a partner or in a small group.

1. Complete the chart with the names of family members who are similar to you in appearance or character. Then share your answers.

How I Am Similar to People in My Family

Characteristic	Family Member's Name and Relationship
Face (for example, eyes, nose, mouth)	
Body size and shape (for example, height, weight)	
Character (for example, shy, funny)	
Other?	

2. Look at the chapter title and the illustrations. Make a list of questions you think "The Science of Genetics" might answer.

a. <u>What is a gene?</u>

b. _____

c. _____

d. _____

B The **boldfaced** words and phrases in the sentences below appear in the reading. Which words are new to you? Circle them. Then, work with a partner. Read the sentences about the reading, and choose the correct answers.

1. We get many **traits** from our parents. Eye color and height are two examples. *Traits* are

   a. gifts.   **b.** qualities.   **c.** interests.

2. If someone has a genetic **disease**, it means that his or her genes are not working correctly, so they have health problems. *Disease* means

   a. sickness.   **b.** trouble.   **c.** fever.

3. Doctors can **prevent** some types of sicknesses by changing the person's genes. When they are successful, people don't get these sicknesses. *Prevent* means

   a. begin doing something.   **b.** stop something   **c.** fix completely.
                                        before it happens.

4. In the future, scientists will try to **get rid of** genes that cause sickness. This would be the best solution because people would never worry about these sicknesses again. *Get rid of* means to cause something to

   a. become smaller.   **b.** get better.   **c.** disappear.

5. Children look like their parents because they **inherit** genes from them. *Inherit* means

   a. receive.   **b.** require.   **c.** get money.

READING

Read the text once without stopping.

The Science of Genetics

1   Who are we? Where did we come from? How are we related to each other and to other living things? The written record of the search for the answers to these questions goes back at least 2,500 years. At that time, Pythagoras, the famous Greek mathematician,[1] believed that children got all of their physical **traits** from their fathers. Later, Aristotle, the Greek philosopher,[2] **realized** that children **inherit** characteristics from both of their parents. However, he incorrectly believed that a child was the direct product of the mixing of the mother's and father's blood.

2   Modern genetics, the science that helps us to understand how and why we get traits from our parents, was not born until the nineteenth century. The father of modern genetics was Gregor Mendel, an Austrian scientist. Through eight years of experiments on pea[3] plants, Mendel proved that characteristics from the "mother" plant and characteristics from the "father" plant are not mixed together when the two plants cross-pollinate[4] and produce the next **generation** of plants. Rather, the characteristics that are dominant (stronger) will **come out** in the first generation. The characteristics that are recessive (weaker) will only appear in the second generation.

3   For example, if you take a very short pea plant and cross-pollinate it with a very tall pea plant, you might expect the new pea plant to be of average height. But in fact, the first generation of plants will all be very tall, because that characteristic is dominant. Short plants will not appear until the second generation, because that characteristic is recessive.

4   The theories that Mendel developed using plants were later applied to all living things, including human beings. Future research that would explain how parents pass traits on[5] to their children through their **genes** grew out of Mendel's work.

5   What is a gene? Explained very simply, a gene is a set of **instructions** that you get from your parents before you are born. Your

continued

---

[1] a *mathematician* = someone who studies or teaches mathematics
[2] a *philosopher* = someone who teaches about life and what it means, and how we should live
[3] a *pea* = a small round green seed that is cooked and eaten as a vegetable
[4] *cross-pollinate* = transfer of pollen (a powder produced by plants) from one plant to another
[5] *pass traits on* = give someone or something a particular trait

genes are similar to an instruction book for a computer. When you open the book, you see a list of all of the parts of the computer. Then, you see instructions telling you how to make the computer work. Your genes, like the instruction book, contain a complete list of all of the parts that make a human being. They also contain instructions on how to put the parts together to make one special **individual**—you.

6   Today, scientists are learning more and more about genes and their effect on what we look like, how we behave, how smart we are, and what kinds of sicknesses we have or are likely to get in the future. They are using this information in two exciting areas: *genetic engineering* and *genetic testing*.

7   Through genetic engineering, scientists change how genes work, or put new genes into **cells** to **replace** genes that are missing or not working correctly. Because all living things (not only humans) have genes, scientists also use genetic engineering to produce plants and animals that are healthy, grow rapidly, or are useful to us in some other way.

8   When doctors do genetic testing, they take DNA[6] from a person (or other living thing) and examine it carefully. One important use of genetic testing is to discover if someone has or might get a genetic **illness**. If the person already has the **disease**, doctors might be able to use genetic engineering to **cure** it. If the testing shows that the person does not have the disease, but might get it at some point in the future, doctors might be able to use genetic engineering to **prevent** it. The treatment involves taking out the gene that causes the disease, and injecting[7] the patient with healthy genes.

9   Sometimes, genetic testing and genetic engineering can be used to **determine** a child's **gender**. In the future, genetic engineering might be used to allow parents to choose **desirable** traits or **get rid of** undesirable ones before their child is even born.

---

[6] *DNA* = deoxyribonucleic acid, an acid that carries genetic information in a cell
[7] *inject* = put a liquid, especially a drug, into the body by using a special needle

Comprehension Check

Read these sentences. Circle T (true) or F (false). If you circle F, change the sentence to make it true. Check your answers with a classmate. If your answers are different, look back at the reading.

1. Around 2,500 years ago people already knew that children   T   F
     get their traits from both their mother and their father.

2. The study of how and why certain traits are passed from   T   F
     one generation to the next is called *genetics*.

3. People look different from one another because they have different genes.　　T　F

4. Our genes do not have an effect on our behavior.　　T　F

5. Genetic engineering is used only on animals.　　T　F

6. In some cases, doctors use genetic testing to find out if someone is sick, or to find out if they might get sick in the future.　　T　F

EXPLORING VOCABULARY

Thinking about the Vocabulary

Guessing Strategy

When writers use technical terms, you might not need to guess their meaning because those terms are often defined directly in the reading itself. Look at the example.

> Rather, the characteristics that are **dominant (stronger)** will come out in the first generation. The characteristics that are **recessive (weaker)** will only appear in the second generation.

Pay attention to words in parentheses. They often contain definitions of the words that come before them.

Try It!

Read the sentence and answer the question.

> Many scientists are doing research in gene therapy (treatment using the part of a cell that carries inherited traits).

What is **gene therapy?** _____

Look at the target words and phrases. Which ones are new to you? Circle them here and in the reading. Then read "The Science of Genetics" again. Look at the context of each new word and phrase. Can you guess the meaning? Use the Guessing Strategy where possible.

Target Words and Phrases

traits (1)	**genes** (4)	**illness** (8)	**determine** (9)
realized (1)	**instructions** (5)	**disease** (8)	**gender** (9)
inherit (1)	**individual** (5)	**cure** (8)	**desirable** (9)
generation (2)	**cells** (7)	**prevent** (8)	**get rid of** (9)
come out (2)	**replace** (7)		

Using the Vocabulary

These sentences are **about the reading**. Complete them with the words and phrases in the box. Circle the words or phrases in the sentences that help you understand the meanings of the target words.

cell	come out	cure	desirable	determine
gender	generation	genes	illnesses	individual
instructions	realize	replace		

1. A long time ago, people didn't know why children tended to look like their parents. They didn't _____ that traits are passed from one _____ to the next.

2. Today, we know that our _____ contain all of the information that is necessary to make a human being. They contain a list of detailed _____ on how to "build" a human being.

3. One _____ is different from another because each person has his or her own genes.

4. The science of genetics (the study of how traits are passed from one generation to another) has shown that some traits will appear in the first generation. Other weaker traits will not _____ until the following generation.

5. Through genetic engineering (changing or replacing genes), doctors are trying to help people with genetic _____ get better. They are trying to _____ them.

6. In one technique, scientists remove a gene that is not working correctly from a _____ (the smallest part of a person or other living thing). Then they _____ it with a healthy gene.

7. It is also possible for scientists to use genetic testing to determine a child's _____ (sex).

8. Genetic testing can be used to _____ (find out) whether a child is likely to develop a genetic illness.

9. In the future, parents might be able to make sure that their children are born with _____ traits such as intelligence or beauty.

DEVELOPING READING SKILLS

Scanning

Where is the information about these topics in "The Science of Genetics"? Scan the reading, and write the paragraph number (1–9).

_____ **a.** The birth of modern genetics

_____ **b.** The definition of a gene

_____ **c.** Possible future uses of genetic engineering and genetic testing

___1___ **d.** Some past ideas about how humans get their traits

_____ **e.** How genetic engineering can be used with animals and plants

_____ **f.** What scientists are learning about genes

_____ **g.** What happens when you cross a small pea plant with a tall one

_____ **h.** How later scientists used Mendel's research

_____ **i.** How genetic testing and genetic engineering are used today in humans

Summarizing

When you **summarize** a text, you should include the main idea and the major points about the main idea. Your summary should include details only if they help you explain the major points. Always write a summary in your own words. Do not copy from the text.

Write a sentence about each of the nine topics from the Scanning exercise above. Use information from the reading, but do not copy. Include only the most important information. Together, the nine sentences should summarize the reading.

Paragraph 1: <u>In the past, there were many different theories about why</u>
               <u>children look and act like their parents.</u>

Paragraph 2: _____

Paragraph 3: _____

Paragraph 4: _____

Paragraph 5: _____

Paragraph 6: _____

Paragraph 7: _____

Paragraph 8: _____

Paragraph 9: _____

EXPANDING VOCABULARY

Using the Vocabulary in New Contexts

These sentences use the target words and phrases **in new contexts.**
Complete them with the words and phrases in the box.

cells	came out	cured	desirable	determines
genders	generations	genes	illness	individual
instructions	realize	replace		

1. This radio isn't working. You need to _____ the batteries.

2. I don't know how to play that game. Please read the _____ to me.

3. Great news! He isn't going to die. The doctors have _____ him!

4. That house is expensive because it is in a _____ location, in the best part of town.

5. Sometimes, parents and children don't understand each other because they come from different _____.

6. The men in his family have been tennis champions for generations. The talent must be in their _____.

7. Doctors now realize that depression is an _____, with real physical causes.

8. I'm sorry. I didn't _____ that I hurt you.

9. Each _____ in the class must participate in at least one experiment.

10. Everyone has two types of blood _____: red and white.

11. The mechanic will call you when he _____ the cause of the problem.

12. Everyone was surprised when the news of his marriage _____. Nobody knew that he had a girlfriend.

13. Most schools in my country are coeducational. That is, they accept students of both _____.

Word Families

Ⓐ Complete the chart with the correct forms of the words. Check your answers in your dictionary. Be careful; you will not use all the words.

Noun	Verb	Adjective
		desirable
	prevent	
	cure	

Ⓑ Complete the sentences with words from the chart.

1. Sicknesses caused by insects are _____. If you protect yourself from insect bites, you won't get these sicknesses.

2. Don't worry. She's not going to die from that disease. It is

   _____.

3. His _____ to become a scientist is so strong that he spends every minute studying and conducting experiments.

4. Scientists are working hard to find a _____ for that disease.

5. The _____ of forest fires is the responsibility of the Department of Fire Safety.

6. Their father gives them whatever they _____.

Ⓒ Working with a partner, answer the questions. Make sure you use the correct form of the **boldfaced** words.

1. Sometimes your **desires** for the future do not match the **desires** of your family or other people that you love. What would you do if this happened to you? Whose **desires** would be more important?

2. Make a list of diseases that are **preventable**. Talk about how you can **prevent** them.

3. Which diseases do you think scientists will find a **cure** for in your lifetime?

Studying Collocations

Certain prepositions follow certain verbs. Sometimes the preposition comes directly after the verb, and sometimes it comes after the object of the verb. In these sentences, the preposition comes after the object.

- He **prevented** us **from** finding out the truth.
- The doctor **cured** her **of** cancer.
- She **inherited** a lot of money **from** her grandmother.
- I damaged her computer, but I **replaced** it **with** a new one.

Write answers to these questions. Use the boldfaced words in your answers.

1. If you have children, what will you try to **prevent** them **from** doing?

   _____

   _____

2. Do you know anyone who has been **cured of** a serious disease?

   _____

   _____

3. Who will **inherit** your money and property **from** you?

   _____

   _____

4. Write about a time when you broke or lost something that belonged to someone else and you had to replace it. What did you **replace** it **with**?

   _____

   _____

PUTTING IT ALL TOGETHER

Discussion

Share your ideas in a small group. As you talk, try to use the vocabulary below. Each time someone uses a target word or phrase, put a check (✓) next to it.

come out	desire/desirable/undesirable	determine	disease
gene/genetic	generation	get rid of	illness
individual	inherit	prevent/preventable	trait

1. Decide which of the following news stories are true. Be ready to explain your answers to the class. After you have discussed all of the news stories, your teacher will tell you which ones are true.

   - Most farmers in the United States use special seeds to grow food. The genes of these seeds have been changed. The plants that grow from them grow faster and are larger than the plants grown from regular seeds. The plants also get fewer diseases.

   - Scientists are now able to take a few cells from a human heart, and grow a new heart from them. This new heart can then be used to replace the heart of someone with heart disease.

   - Scientists are now using genetic engineering to produce pigs with livers that are genetically the same as human livers. In the future, doctors hope to be able to replace the diseased livers of human beings with these pig livers.

   - Scientists have discovered the gene for intelligence. Parents can now use genetic testing before their baby is born to find out whether their child is going to be intelligent or not.

2. Choose one of the true news stories above and talk about it in your group. Do you think using genetic engineering and/or testing in this way is a good thing or a bad thing? Why?

Writing

Complete one or both of these writing topics. When you write, use at least five of the target words from the chapter. Underline the target words in your paper.

1. Genetic testing now makes it possible for people to find out if they have a higher than average chance of getting certain genetic diseases. Write a paragraph or short essay discussing the advantages and disadvantages of knowing this information. You can start with the following sentence: *There are both advantages and disadvantages to knowing if you have a high risk for getting a genetic disease.*

2. Imagine that you are a manager at a large insurance company. You find out that very soon everyone who applies to your company for health insurance will be given a genetic test to determine how likely they are to develop a genetic illness. The test will tell you which people are most likely to develop a serious genetic disease in the future. In an e-mail to the other managers of the company, explain why you agree or disagree with this use of genetic testing.

CHAPTER 8

Designing the Future

Designer babies?

GETTING READY TO READ

  First, answer the questions alone. Then compare your answers with a partner or in a small group.

1. Look at the list of adjectives. If you could choose only three for your **son**, which would you choose and why? Put a check (✓) next to three, or write in your own.

   _____ strong   _____ thin   _____ handsome   _____ honest

   _____ intelligent   _____ funny   _____ kind   _____ successful

   other? _____

2. Now check the three adjectives that you would choose for your **daughter**.

   _____ strong   _____ thin   _____ beautiful   _____ honest

   _____ intelligent   _____ funny   _____ kind   _____ successful

   other? _____

B The **boldfaced** words in the paragraph below appear in the reading. Which words are new to you? Circle them. Then, work with a partner. Read this paragraph introducing the topic of the reading, and match the words with their definitions.

> **Historically**, parents could only hope that their child would be born with desirable moral traits such as **courage**. However, due to rapid progress in the field of genetics, very soon parents might be able to do much more than hope. They might **actually** be able to "design" their children before they are born. How? Some scientists believe that within the next 50 years, they will be able to **identify** the genes for everything from nose shape to intelligence. And after a gene for a particular **feature** is identified, scientists can use genetic engineering to make sure that a child is born with that trait.

Word	Definition
_____ 1. historically	**a.** the ability to be brave and calm in a situation where most people would be afraid
_____ 2. courage	**b.** traditionally; in the past
_____ 3. actually	**c.** an important and noticeable characteristic of something
_____ 4. identify	**d.** find out exactly what the cause or origin of something is
_____ 5. feature	**e.** in fact, although it may be strange

READING

Read the text once without stopping.

Designing the Future

1   A young couple has decided that it is time for them to have a baby. So, what is the first thing they do? They go shopping! But not for clothes or furniture—that will come later. Before anything else, they must decide whether they want a girl or a boy. Now, it is time to consider their future child's **intellect**. Do they want an intellectually gifted child, or would a child with an average level of intelligence be **acceptable**? Next, what about personality? Is **courage** important to them? Do they care if their child is shy? Finally, it is time to consider physical traits. What eye color would they prefer? What about height and weight? Do they want an

continued

athletic child, so that he or she can play tennis with Mom? There are so many **features** to choose from!

2   Of course, the situation described above does not **actually** happen today. But recent progress in genetic engineering[1] has **led** some scientists **to** believe that the day when parents can "shop" for their future child's physical, intellectual, and personality traits is rapidly **approaching**. It seems that almost every day scientists **identify** new genes and the traits that they control. Already, genetic testing can be used to identify gender very early in the development of the fetus.[2] The genes that mark for[3] a few serious genetic diseases can also be identified. And there are scientists who are convinced that very soon they will find the genes for a wide variety of traits—artistic talent, courage, a tendency toward depression, physical **appearance**—just about anything you can imagine. Reportedly, one scientist has even spoken of using genetic engineering to give future humans desirable traits that only animals have now—for example, a dog's powerful sense of smell, or an owl's[4] ability to see at night.

3   However, not everyone working in the field of genetics believes that parents will be making such choices anytime soon. Some believe that the more complex types of genetic engineering will not be possible for at least 100 years. Others are not at all **convinced** that our genes control characteristics such as intelligence and personality. And still others believe that the use of genetic engineering should be **restricted** to just those cases in which the health of the mother or her fetus is threatened.

4   Surveys show that the attitudes of the public on this subject have been changing, at least in the United States. In a telephone survey done in the United States in 1986, 42 percent thought that changing the genes of human cells was morally wrong. However, in the same survey done in 1996, that number had dropped to only 22 percent. Other recent surveys have shown that many parents would be willing to use genetic engineering to improve their child's chances of inheriting desirable traits, such as beauty or intelligence. And it is instructive to remember that **historically**, whenever the once unimaginable has become possible (think about cars, airplanes, and the Internet), it soon becomes common. That is why many believe that if the technology to "design" children exists, parents will use it in ever increasing numbers.

continued

----

[1] *genetic engineering* = the science of changing the genes of a plant or animal to make it stronger or more healthy

[2] a *fetus* = a young human or animal before birth

[3] *mark for* = signal or show the presence of (something)

[4] an *owl* = a bird that hunts at night and has large eyes and a loud call

5   All of this **brings up** some difficult social and moral questions. What are the long-term[5] health risks of genetic engineering? Will too many parents choose to have children of the same gender leading to a **shortage** of boys or girls? What will happen to children whose parents cannot afford to give them the physical and mental **advantages** enjoyed by their genetically "designed" peers? How will society treat "imperfect" children? **In short**, will genetic engineering forever change the face of **humanity**?

_____

[5] *long-term* = continuing for a long period of time into the future

Comprehension Check

Read these sentences. Circle T (true), F (false) or ? (can't determine the answer from the reading). If you circle F, change the sentence to make it true. Check your answers with a classmate. If your answers are different, look back at the reading.

1. Intelligence and personality are determined by our genes.   T   F   ?

2. It is now possible for parents to determine the sex of their   T   F   ?
   child before it is born.

3. Some parents are already using genetic engineering to   T   F   ?
   determine what their future child will look like.

4. In the future, some scientists expect to find the genes for   T   F   ?
   almost all the traits that are passed from parents to their
   children.

5. Even if genetic engineering makes it possible for parents   T   F   ?
   to "design" their children, most parents won't use the
   technology because it is morally wrong.

6. Genetic engineering to change children's physical   T   F   ?
   appearance will have no effect on their health.

EXPLORING VOCABULARY

Thinking about the Vocabulary

Guessing Strategy

Understanding punctuation can help you understand the meaning of unfamiliar words. The **dash** (—) is a type of punctuation. Writers use dashes to focus the reader's attention on important information. Often, writers put examples between two dashes. Look at the example.

And there are scientists who are convinced that very soon they will find the genes for a wide variety of traits—artistic talent, **courage**, a tendency toward depression, physical **appearance**—just about anything you can imagine.

In this case, the word before the dash is *traits.* The words after the dash are specific examples of different kinds of traits. Although you may not understand the exact meaning of the target words *courage* or *appearance,* you can guess from the context that they are both traits.

Try It!

Read the sentence, and write a definition of the **boldfaced** target word.

Genetic engineering brings up serious social and moral issues—health risks, a possible **shortage** of boys or girls—so many people worry about using it.

Shortage means _____

Look at the target words and phrases. Which ones are new to you? Circle them here and in the reading. Then read "Designing the Future" again. Look at the context of each new word and phrase. Can you guess the meaning? Use the Guessing Strategy where possible.

Target Words and Phrases			
intellect (1)	actually (2)	convinced (3)	shortage (5)
acceptable (1)	led to (2)	restricted (3)	advantages (5)
courage (1)	approaching (2)	historically (4)	in short (5)
athletic (1)	identify (2)	brings up (5)	humanity (5)
features (1)	appearance (2)		

Using the Vocabulary

These sentences are **about the reading**. Complete them with the words and phrases in the box. Circle the words or phrases in the sentences that help you understand the meanings of the target words.

acceptable	advantages	appearance	approaching	athletic
brings up	convinced	humanity	in short	intellect
lead to	restricted	shortage		

1. Some scientists believe that the day when parents will be able to choose what their future children look like is rapidly _____. Others think that it will take at least 100 years.

2. For some parents, choosing physical traits is important. They would like to be able to determine their children's height, or _____ ability.

3. It might also be possible for parents to determine their child's _____. Some parents will probably want their children to be gifted. Others will be happier with children of average intelligence.

4. People are starting to ask some very difficult questions about genetic engineering. Genetic engineering _____ some complex questions.

5. The technology to determine the gender of the fetus already exists. Some people worry that if too many parents choose one gender, there will be a _____ of the other gender.

6. Many people in the United States think that there is nothing wrong with using genetic engineering to design children with desirable traits. They think that this use of genetic engineering is _____.

7. In the future, parents will probably be able to choose certain traits for their children. The physical traits that the parents choose will have an effect on their child's _____.

8. One scientist believes that we will be able to design people who have both human and animal traits. He doesn't think we will be _____ to just human traits.

9. Although some scientists are _____ that there are genes for almost all traits, others disagree. They don't think that genes control complex personality traits or intellect.

10. Some people are concerned that using genetic engineering to design the perfect child will _____ a society in which rich children have genetic _____ over poor children.

11. They worry that the use of genetic engineering to design babies could change the definition of what a human being is. _____, they worry that genetic engineering will have a negative effect on _____.

DEVELOPING READING SKILLS

Understanding Inference

Read the sentences from "Designing the Future." Then, read the two sentences that follow. Put a check (✓) next to the sentence in each set that is a reasonable inference based on the sentences from the reading. The numbers in parentheses are the paragraphs that the sentences come from.

1. But recent progress in genetic engineering has led some scientists to believe that the day when parents can "shop" for their future child's physical, intellectual, and personality traits is rapidly approaching. (2)

   _____ The technology for designing babies does not exist yet.

   _____ In the future, almost all parents will design their babies.

2. Reportedly, one scientist has even spoken of using genetic engineering to give future humans desirable traits that only animals have now. (2)

   _____ Human beings will soon be able to have traits that only animals have now.

   _____ Right now, scientists don't know how to make humans with animal traits.

3. However, not everyone working in the field of genetics believes that parents will be making such choices anytime soon. (3)

   _____ Nobody working in genetics believes that parents will want to choose their children's traits.

   _____ Some geneticists think that it will be a long time before the technology that will allow parents to design their babies is developed.

Summarizing

Complete this summary of "Designing the Future." Write as much as you can without looking back at the reading. Then, compare your summary to that of a classmate. If there are any differences, decide whose summary is more accurate. Finally, go back to the reading to check your summary and to add any missing information.

Because of genetic _____, many scientists believe

that in the future, parents will be able to _____.

Already, scientists know how to _____. In the

future, scientists expect to _____. When that

happens, surveys show that many parents _____.

The use of genetic engineering to "design" children leads to some difficult moral questions, for example: _____? But the

most important question is: _____?

EXPANDING VOCABULARY

Using the Vocabulary in New Contexts

These sentences use the target words and phrases **in new contexts**.
Complete them with the words and phrases in the box.

acceptable	advantages	appearance	approach	athletic
bring up	convinced	humanity	in short	intellect
lead to	restricted	shortage		

1. He can't throw a ball or run fast. He isn't very _____.

2. I had a lot of homework to do, but my sister _____ me to go
   to the movies with her.

3. The work of Austrian scientist Gregor Mendel, the father of genetics, was
   important for all of _____.

4. You look different. Your new haircut really changes your

   _____.

5. Travel to that region is _____. You can only go there if you get
   permission from the government.

6. Bad eating habits can _____ illness and other physical
   problems.

7. I'm sorry, but this paper is not _____. It is very messy and has
   many errors. You are going to have to write it again.

8. You should _____ your concerns in class. Your teacher will
   help you.

9. There is nothing wrong with her _____. She's a very smart
   woman.

10. There are many _____ to having a good education. For
    example, people who are well-educated usually earn more money than
    people with less education.

11. He is attractive, intelligent, and successful. _____, he's the perfect man for you!

12. It hasn't rained in almost a year. There is a water _____.

13. Slow down as we _____ the traffic light. My house is on the corner, just after the light.

Word Families

The adjective ending *-ous* means "full of." Therefore, the adjective *courageous* means "full of courage." The addition of certain suffixes, including *-ous*, can change the syllable stress on a word. Your dictionary will tell you which syllable to stress when you add a suffix.

A **Look at the pronunciation guides for the following words. Answer the questions.**

1.
> **cour·age** /ˈkɚɪdʒ, ˈkʌr-/ *n*
> **cou·ra·geous** /kəˈreɪdʒəs/ *adj*

a. How many syllables are in the noun **courage**? _____
Which syllable is stressed? _____

b. How many syllables are in the adjective **courageous**? _____
Which syllable is stressed? _____

2.
> **ad·van·tage** /ədˈvæntɪdʒ/ *n*
> **ad·van·ta·geous** /ˌædvænˈteɪdʒəs, -vən-/ *adj*

a. How many syllables are in the noun **advantage**? _____
Which syllable is stressed? _____

b. How many syllables are in the adjective **advantageous**?
_____
Which syllable is stressed? _____

3.
> **anx·i·e·ty** /æŋˈzaɪəti/ *n*
> **anx·ious** /ˈæŋkʃəs, ˈæŋʃəs/ *adj*

a. How many syllables are in the noun **anxiety**? _____
Which syllable is stressed? _____

b. How many syllables are in the adjective **anxious**? _____
Which syllable is stressed? _____

B Working with a partner, answer the questions. Use the **boldfaced** words in your answers. Make sure you stress the correct syllable.

1. When you feel **anxious**, what do you do to relax?

2. In life, which is more **advantageous**—physical beauty or intellectual ability? Why?

3. Are you a **courageous** person? Explain your answer with specific examples.

Studying Word Grammar

An **adverb** is a word that can be used to modify a verb, an adjective, another adverb, or an entire sentence. Look at the examples.

They lost the game despite fighting **courageously** up until the very end.	The adverb *courageously* modifies the verb *fighting*.
It is important for children to be **intellectually** challenged.	The adverb *intellectually* modifies the adjective *challenged*.
My son is **very** athletically gifted.	The adverb *very* modifies the adverb *athletically*.
Historically, whenever the once unimaginable has become possible, it soon becomes common.	The adverb *historically* modifies the whole sentence that follows it.

Complete the sentences with the adverbs below.

actually   historically   humanely   in short

1. _____, women stayed at home and took care of the children. Today, however, many women work outside of the home.

2. It is not acceptable to hurt an animal on purpose. Animals should be treated _____.

3. Your artwork is creative, original, intelligent, and beautiful. _____, it's remarkable!

4. Most people think he's been playing the piano for years. _____, he just began playing three months ago.

PUTTING IT ALL TOGETHER

Discussion

Share your ideas in a small group. As you talk, try to use the vocabulary below. Each time someone uses a target word or phrase, put a check (✓) next to it.

acceptable	advantage/advantageous	appearance
athletic	courage/courageous	feature
humanity	identify	intellect/intellectual
lead to	restricted	shortage

1. Imagine that in the future you will be able to design your own son or daughter. Will you do it? Why or why not?
2. Read the last paragraph on page 99 again, and discuss your answers to the five questions.

Writing

Complete one or both of these writing topics. When you write, use at least five of the target words from the chapter. Underline the target words in your paper.

1. Imagine that in the future you will be able to design your own child. What traits do you want your son or daughter to have? Write a letter to your future child explaining why you wanted him or her to have these traits.
2. *The use of genetic engineering to make a child more intelligent or more attractive is morally wrong.* Do you agree or disagree with this statement? Write a short essay explaining your opinion.

CHAPTER 9

A Drug to Match Your Genes

"Do you have a drug to match my genes?"

GETTING READY TO READ

 Talk with a partner or in a small group.

1. When you are sick, do you usually take medicine?
2. Have you ever taken medicine that made you sick? What happened?
3. When you have a headache, do you take any medicine for the pain? Do some pain medicines work better for you than others? Have you ever taken a medicine that worked well for someone else, but did not have any effect on you?

B The **boldfaced** words and phrases in the sentences below appear in the reading. Which words are new to you? Circle them. Then, work with a partner. Read the sentences about the reading, and choose the correct answers.

1. If you are sick, your doctor might **prescribe** some medicine to help you **recover**. *Prescribe* means

   a. mix together.   **b.** write an order for.   **c.** invent.

2. When you *recover* from an illness, you

   a. get better.   **b.** get weaker.   **c.** get help.

3. After an **operation**, most people take medicine to help them deal with the pain. An *operation* is

   a. a medical procedure involving cutting into the body.
   b. a long and severe illness.
   c. a serious mental condition.

4. If you are **fortunate**, the medicine will work for you. A *fortunate* person is

   a. lucky.
   b. happy.
   c. healthy.

5. If the drug works as the doctor **intended** it to work, you will feel better. If doctors *intend* for something to work, they

   a. expect that it will be successful.
   b. write an order for it.
   c. study for it.

6. It is possible for a drug to be **beneficial** for one person, but dangerous for another. A *beneficial* drug is

   a. helpful.
   b. difficult.
   c. strong.

READING

Read the text once without stopping.

A Drug to Match Your Genes

1   Everyone has probably had the experience of going into a clothing store to find a shirt to match a favorite skirt or pair of pants. But imagine what it would be like if you could go into a pharmacy and ask for a medication to match your genes. Scientists in the field of personalized medicine hope that one day doctors will be able to match their patients' medications to their genetic makeup[1] as easily as a salesperson helps a customer find the perfect shirt to match his jeans.

2   To understand how personalized medicine (also called *pharmacogenomics*) works, think about how doctors currently decide which medicines to **prescribe** for their patients. When you go into your doctor's office complaining of a problem, your doctor will most likely prescribe a medication that has been **effective** for a large number of people. However, the fact that it works for many others does not mean that it will be **beneficial** for you. And in the worst case, it could even be **harmful** to your health. In fact, hundreds of thousands of people enter the hospital every year because of bad reactions to medicines that their doctors prescribed for them, and many die.

continued

---

[1] *genetic makeup* = the genes that you inherit from your parents

3   Does this mean that there was something wrong with these drugs, or that the doctor made a mistake, or that the patients took the drug incorrectly? In many cases, the answer is no. A variety of **factors** can affect how you react to a drug, including your age, how **severe** your disease is, your **diet**, and any other drugs you are taking. But the most important factor is your genes.

4   Why is a medicine that is so effective for one individual so harmful to another? When a drug enters someone's body, the person's genes control the drug's action. Genes control how much of the drug will be active and available for the body to use, and how much will be inactive. One person's genes, for example, might make only 20 percent of the drug active, with 80 percent inactive. With the same dose[2] of the same medicine, another person's genes might make 98 percent of the dose active, and only 2 percent inactive.

5   Genes are also **in charge of** how quickly a drug works on the part of the body for which it was **intended**. Imagine three women—Barbara, Elizabeth, and Claudia—all **suffering** from the same disease. Their doctor has prescribed the same dose of the same drug for all three of them. Barbara is lucky. Her genes allow her body to use the correct amount of the drug in the correct amount of time, and it works well for her. In other words, she has a positive reaction to the drug. Elizabeth, however, is not quite as **fortunate**. Her genes cause her body to use the drug so quickly that it has no time to provide any benefit. Therefore, the drug is not effective for Elizabeth. Claudia, unfortunately, is in trouble. She is one of the 10 percent of Caucasians[3] and 20 percent of Asians who, due to their genetic makeup, have trouble metabolizing[4] drugs. This means that Claudia's body uses drugs very slowly. The high levels of a drug in her blood over a long period of time can **poison** her.

6   Individual genetic differences also explain why medicines that doctors prescribe for pain perform differently in different patients. Two people of the same age, height, and weight who are **recovering** from the same **operation** can be given exactly the same drug to control their pain, yet have completely different reactions. For example, one study in the United States showed that the drug codeine, which is one of the most commonly prescribed pain medications, has no effect on about 20 million Americans. Currently, however, the only way most people find out that a drug is ineffective or even dangerous for them is when they try it the first time. For some, sadly, there will be no second chance.

7   Fortunately, research into personalized medicine is **progressing** rapidly. The day when your doctor will be able to prescribe a drug to fit your individual body chemistry may not be so far away.

---

[2] a *dose* = a measured amount of medicine

[3] a *Caucasian* = belonging to the race that has pale, or white, skin

[4] *metabolize* = When your body **metabolizes** a food or drug, the food or drug is chemically changed so that it can be used by your body.

Comprehension Check

Read these sentences. Circle T (true) or F (false). If you circle F, change the sentence to make it true. Check your answers with a classmate. If your answers are different, look back at the reading.

1. The same medicine can have a completely different effect on two different people.   T   F

2. The food that you eat can have an effect on the way that your body reacts to a drug.   T   F

3. The way that your body uses a drug depends on your genes.   T   F

4. Children and adults probably have different reactions to the same drug.   T   F

5. Doctors can now give a patient a drug that is designed just for him or her, not for any other person.   T   F

6. Sometimes, people of different racial backgrounds have different reactions to the same drug.   T   F

EXPLORING VOCABULARY

Thinking about the Vocabulary

Guessing Strategy

Antonyms are words that have opposite meanings. Look at the example.

> Two children with the same disease receive the same medicine: one child **recovers**; the other dies.

The contrast in this sentence is between the two verbs *recover* and *die*. They are antonyms. If you understand the meaning of *die*, you can guess that *recover* has an opposite meaning.

Try It!

Read the sentence, and write a definition of the **boldfaced** target word.

> Eating the right kinds of food is **beneficial** to your health, but eating too much can be bad for you.

Beneficial means _____

Look at the target words and phrases. Which ones are new to you? Circle them here and in the reading. Then read "A Drug to Match Your Genes" again. Look at the context of each new word and phrase. Can you guess the meaning? Use the Guessing Strategy where possible.

Target Words and Phrases

prescribe (2)	factors (3)	intended (5)	recovering (6)
effective (2)	severe (3)	suffering (5)	operation (6)
beneficial (2)	diet (3)	fortunate (5)	progressing (7)
harmful (2)	in charge of (5)	poison (5)	

Using the Vocabulary

These sentences are **about the reading**. Complete them with the words and phrases in the box. Circle the words or phrases in the sentences that help you understand the meanings of the target words.

diet	effective	factor	harmful	in charge of
poison	progressing	severe	suffer	

1. One important _____ that affects how well a drug works in your body is your age.

2. What, how, and how much you eat can also have an effect on the way you feel after you take a drug. In other words, your _____ has an important effect on the way your body uses drugs.

3. The effect a drug has on your body also depends on how serious your disease is. If you _____ from a _____ illness, certain drugs may not work very well for you.

4. The same medicine can be safe for one person, but very _____ for another.

5. Also, two individuals might need different amounts of medicine. An amount of medicine that is _____ for one person can _____, and even kill, another person.

6. Our genes control our reactions to medicine. Genes are _____ whether or not we react positively to a drug.

7. Research into personalized medicine is _____ very rapidly. Soon, doctors might be able to prescribe drugs that exactly fit an individual's body chemistry.

DEVELOPING READING SKILLS

Understanding Supporting Details

Reread "A Drug to Match Your Genes." Check (✓) the correct answer, and underline the place in the text where you found the information. If the reading doesn't give the information, check "It doesn't say."

	Yes	No	It doesn't say
1. Does the way you live have an effect on how you react to a drug?	☐	☐	☐
2. If a small amount of a drug works well for you, will a larger dose work even better?	☐	☐	☐
3. If you take a larger amount of a drug than your doctor prescribes for you, will it definitely poison you?	☐	☐	☐
4. Are drug companies giving a lot of money to the government for research into personalized medicine?	☐	☐	☐
5. Is the drug codeine effective for everyone?	☐	☐	☐
6. Can your race have an effect on your reaction to a drug?	☐	☐	☐

Understanding Major Points

Talk with a partner. Answer these questions. Do not look back at the reading. After you finish talking, write down your answers as completely as you can. Don't worry about grammar or spelling. Just focus on putting the major points into your own words.

1. Why does the same medicine affect two people differently? Give more than one reason.

_____

_____

2. What is the most important reason that different people react differently to the same drug?

   _____

   _____

3. Explain the connection between genes and what happens inside the body when you take a drug.

   _____

   _____

4. In the future, how might the drugs that our doctors prescribe for us be different from the drugs we take today?

   _____

   _____

EXPANDING VOCABULARY

Using the Vocabulary in New Contexts

These sentences use the target words and phrases **in new contexts**. Complete them with the words and phrases in the box.

diet	effective	factor	harmful	in charge of
poison	progressed	severe	suffering	

1. You are eating too much. It isn't healthy. You need to change your

   _____.

2. Sitting too close to a television when you are watching it can be

   _____ to your eyes.

3. He has _____ very quickly in his career. He has been at the company for only one year, but he's already in charge of three departments and 100 employees.

4. She saw mice in her apartment, so she is going to get something to

   _____ them.

5. There is going to be a _____ snowstorm tonight. I think we should stay home.

6. He's a very _____ teacher. His students always learn a lot from him.

7. Her job is very important. She is _____ 1,000 workers.

8. He is _____ from cancer, but fortunately, the type that he has is curable.

9. One _____ to consider when buying a car is the cost.

Word Families

A Read these sentences, and write the target words that are in the same word families as the **boldfaced** words.

1. The patient's **recovery** was much faster than his doctors had expected.

   Target word: _____

2. She had a bad cough, so her doctor wrote her a **prescription** for cough medicine.

   Target word: _____

3. I'm sorry. It was never my **intention** to hurt you.

   Target word: _____

4. I know my dog looks scary, but he would never bite anyone. He's **harmless**.

   Target word: _____

5. In this book, there is a **progression** of activities from easy to more difficult.

   Target word: _____

B Match the words from Exercise A to their definitions. Be careful; there is one extra definition.

_____ 1. recovery

_____ 2. prescription

_____ 3. intention

_____ 4. harmless

_____ 5. progression

a. a change or development from one situation or state to another

b. not dangerous

c. the act of getting better after an illness

d. something that you plan to do

e. the patient who a doctor operates on

f. a piece of paper from your doctor that says which medicine you need and allows you to get it

Studying Collocations

Medicine, like any professional field, has specialized vocabulary that includes many collocations. Look at the **boldfaced** collocations in the examples.

- She **suffers from** high blood pressure.
- She is in the hospital, **recovering from** a serious illness.
- He has very high cholesterol, so he has to **follow a strict diet**.
- The doctor who **performed the operation** made a serious mistake.

Ⓐ Rewrite the following sentences with the correct collocations. Write one word in each space.

1. My father has skin cancer.

   My father _____ _____ skin cancer.

2. After his illness, he got better in a week.

   He _____ _____ _____

   _____ in a week.

3. Dr. Smith will be in charge of the operation.

   Dr. Smith will _____ _____ _____ .

4. His doctor told him to be very careful about what he eats.

   His doctor advised him to _____ _____

   _____ _____ .

Ⓑ Write answers to these questions. Use the **boldfaced** collocations in your answers.

1. If you were **suffering from an incurable illness**, would you want your doctor to tell you, or would you rather not know?

   _____

   _____

2. Why do children usually **recover from an illness** more quickly than elderly people?

   _____

   _____

3. Have you ever watched a doctor **perform an operation**? If so, describe it. If not, would you like to? Why or why not?

   _____

   _____

4. People who suffer from certain diseases have to **follow a strict diet**. Name a couple of these diseases, and make a list of the foods that are restricted for each one.

_____

_____

PUTTING IT ALL TOGETHER

Discussion

Share your ideas in a small group. As you talk, try to use the vocabulary below. Each time someone uses a target word or phrase, put a check (✓) next to it.

beneficial	effective	factor	fortunate	harmful
prescribe	progress	recover	severe	suffer from

1. "A Drug to Match Your Genes" talks about one way that genetic testing can help us. However, some people think that genetic testing can be dangerous. They worry that we don't know who will use the information and how they will use it. For example, a company might want you to get a genetic test before they will give you a job. Then, depending on the results of the test, they will decide whether to give you a job or not. Do you think companies should be allowed to do this?

2. Imagine a day when scientists and doctors will be able to prevent or cure all diseases. Will this be a completely positive thing? Can you imagine any problems that this might lead to?

Writing

Choose one or both of the Discussion questions above to write about. When you write, use at least five of the target words from the chapter. Underline the target words in your paper.

Wrap-up

REVIEWING READING SKILLS AND VOCABULARY

Read the text. Do not use a dictionary.

1   Historically, it took individual farmers generations of experimentation to develop the strongest, healthiest, and fastest-growing variety of a crop. Today, however, due to rapid progress in gene research, farmers can buy seeds whose genes have been carefully changed in a laboratory. The crops that grow from these genetically engineered seeds grow faster and are stronger and less likely to suffer from disease than traditional crops. In short, they have all the traits that farmers used to spend generations developing. The food that is produced from these crops is called genetically modified (GM).

2   In the United States, it is almost impossible to find food that does not contain at least some GM products. Actually, it is very difficult to determine whether you are buying GM food. That is because food labels in the United States do not usually identify products that have been genetically modified. In Western Europe, however, things are very different. Walk into almost any supermarket in France, Great Britain, or Italy, and you will see labels on the food that read "GM-free." By reading the labels, customers can identify those products that have not been genetically modified in any way.

3   Why the difference? Although scientists say that GM food is harmless, many Europeans do not believe it. They express concern about the possible negative effects of growing and eating GM food. They worry about the effect it might have on the health of individuals and the environment. Finally, many Europeans are especially sensitive to this issue because of the importance of food to their culture.

4   In the United States, however, scientists and farmers who produce GM food argue that it is not only harmless but actually beneficial to humanity. They claim that by growing GM crops, farmers can produce much more food in a shorter period of time. In that way, GM products can help prevent hunger in parts of the world suffering from food shortages.

Comprehension Check

Read these sentences. Circle T (true), F (false), or ? (can't determine the answer from the reading). If you circle F, change the sentence to make it true.

1. In the past, farmers had no way to develop healthier, faster-growing plants.   T   F   ?

2. Today, most farmers in the United States benefit from the progress that scientists have made in the field of genetic engineering.   T   F   ?

3. By reading food labels, customers in the United States can decide for themselves whether or not to buy food that contains GM products.   T   F   ?

4. Many western Europeans are worried that GM food could make them sick.   T   F   ?

5. It is difficult to find GM food in Europe today.   T   F   ?

Guessing Meaning from Context

Answer these questions.

1. Look at the word *crops* in paragraph 1. Write some examples of crops.

   _____

2. What is the meaning of the word *modified* in paragraph 1?

   _____

3. Look at the word *labels* in paragraph 2. What information is often written

   on these kinds of labels? _____

Understanding Major Points

Answer these questions about the major points in the reading. Use your own words. Do not copy from the text.

1. What is the definition of genetically modified food?

   _____

   _____

2. What are some of the benefits of genetically modified food?

   _____

   _____

3. What are some of the possible problems with genetically modified food?

   _____

   _____

EXPANDING VOCABULARY

Studying Word Grammar

Some verbs must have a noun immediately after them. This noun is called a **direct object.** Verbs that need a direct object are called **transitive verbs.** The verb "love" is a transitive verb.

                 verb   *direct object*
Transitive: I love   ice cream.

Other verbs do not have a direct object. These verbs are called **intransitive verbs.** The verb "listen" is an intransitive verb: *He is listening to the radio,* or *He is listening.* We can't say *He is listening radio.*

                 verb   *object of the preposition*
Intransitive: He is listening   to the radio.
                He is listening.

Ⓐ **Look at the boldfaced verbs in these sentences. Circle T (transitive verb), or I (intransitive verb).**

1. Their research is **progressing** rapidly.   T   I

2. To **prevent** heart disease, you should eat a healthy diet.   T   I

3. I don't like to see anyone **suffer**.   T   I

4. When his grandmother died, he **inherited** her house.   T   I

Ⓑ **Write your own sentences with the verbs from Exercise A.**

1. _____

2. _____

3. _____

4. _____

Word Families

Look at these sentences.

    Fortunately, your disease is not severe.
    Unfortunately, however, it is **in**curable.

A **prefix** is a word part added to the beginning of a word. It changes the word's meaning. The prefixes *un-* and *in-* both mean *not.* Other common prefixes include *dis-*, which also means *not*, and *mis-*, which means *wrong* or *bad.*

Complete these sentences with your own ideas. There is more than one correct way to complete each sentence.

1. If your father gives you **unrestricted** use of his car, you can

   <u>use it any time you want</u> .

2. If your parents **disinherit** you, you won't _____.

3. If you suffer a **misfortune**, your friends might _____.

4. If your way of doing something is **ineffective**, you should

   _____.

5. If your boss tells you that your work is **unacceptable**, you should

   _____.

PLAYING WITH WORDS

You can play the game Concentration alone, but it is more fun if you play with one, two, or three other students.

- **Step 1:** Choose 10 words from the unit that you are having trouble learning. Take 20 blank index cards, and make 10 cards with just the words written on them, and 10 cards with the definitions of the 10 words written on them.

- **Step 2:** Next, mix the cards up well, and lay them face-down on a large desk or table, four cards across and five cards down.

- **Step 3:** Now, turn over any two cards, and try to remember what is written on them and where they are. If they form a match—a word or phrase on one card, a matching definition on the other—pick them up from the board and keep them, and take another turn. However, leave the other cards exactly where they were. If the two cards you turn over do not match, turn them both back over. Now it's the next person's turn. Play until all of the cards have been matched up. The winner is the person who has the most cards.

BUILDING DICTIONARY SKILLS

Finding Collocations

Your dictionary is an excellent resource for learning collocations. Look carefully at the entire dictionary entry, including the example sentences, for patterns of words that occur together.

 These dictionary entries come from the *Longman Dictionary of American English*. Look carefully at the example sentences in the dictionary, and then complete the sentences below each dictionary entry. Write one word in each space.

Instructions

> **in·struc·tion** /ɪnˈstrʌkʃən/ *n* **1** [C usually plural] information or advice that tells you how to do something, especially printed material that explains how to use a piece of equipment, machine etc.: *Follow the instructions on the back of the box.* | *Don't forget to read the instructions.* | *He gave us* **instructions on/about how to** *fix the toilet.* **2** [U] teaching that you are given in a particular skill or subject: *He's* **under instruction** *to become a pilot.* -**instructional** *adj*

1. _____ the instructions on the label.

Prescribe/prescription

> **pre·scribe** /prɪˈskraɪb/ *v* [T] **1** to say what medicine or treatment a sick person should have: *Dr. Dawson* **prescribed** *some sleeping pills* **for** *me.* **2** FORMAL to state officially what should be done in a particular situation: *a punishment prescribed by the law*
> **pre·scrip·tion** /prɪˈskrɪpʃən/ *n* **1** a piece of paper on which a doctor writes what medicine a sick person should have, or the medicine itself: *a* **prescription for** *his chest pains* **2** an idea or suggestion about how to solve a problem or improve a situation: *What's your* **prescription for** *a happy marriage?*

2. My dentist _____ pain medicine _____ me.

3. My dentist wrote me a _____ _____ pain medicine.

Diet

> **di·et¹** /ˈdaɪət/ *n* **1** [C,U] the type of food that you eat each day: *A healthy diet and exercise are important for good health.* **2** a plan to eat only particular kinds or amounts of food: *a low-fat diet* | *No dessert for me—I'm* **on a diet.** (=trying to become thinner)
> **diet²** *v* [I] to eat less or eat only particular foods in order to lose weight: *Jill's always dieting.*

4. I can't have any ice cream. I am _____ _____

    _____.

B Write your own sentences about yourself and your life with the words from Exercise A.

1. _____

_____

2. _____

_____

3. _____

_____

Vocabulary Self-Test 1

Circle the letter of the word or phrase that best completes each sentence. Example:

Scientists usually work in _____.

a. laboratories   **c.** personalities

b. literature   **d.** victims

1. That performer _____ received $10,000 for just one performance.

   a. rapidly   **c.** morally

   b. reportedly   **d.** historically

2. The scientist conducted some _____ to find out how much sleep most teens need.

   a. experiments   **c.** championships

   b. equipment   **d.** patterns

3. I'm tired because I _____ too late last night.

   a. stayed up   **c.** stood out

   b. grew out of   **d.** burned out

4. The cat _____ her on the face.

   a. scratched   **c.** cured

   b. survived   **d.** prevented

5. Poems often contain words that _____.

   a. spin   **c.** compete

   b. replace   **d.** rhyme

6. That team has won several _____.

   a. complaints   **c.** cells

   b. championships   **d.** features

7. Leave your little brother alone. Don't _____ him.

   a. pick on   **c.** drop out

   b. bring up   **d.** stand up for

8. To be successful, it is important to have high _____.

   a. mystery

   b. self-esteem

   c. concern

   d. diet

9. When your grandmother dies, you are going to _____ this house.

   a. progress

   b. contribute

   c. reduce

   d. inherit

10. The government spends very little money on education. Almost 60 percent of the people in the country are _____.

    a. live

    b. athletic

    c. illiterate

    d. anxious

11. Don't work so hard. You'll _____.

    a. stay up

    b. burn out

    c. in charge of

    d. pick on

12. This is a _____ area. You cannot enter.

    a. talented

    b. remarkable

    c. moral

    d. restricted

13. He is not doing well in school because he has a bad _____.

    a. appearance

    b. individual

    c. attitude

    d. official

14. Stay in school. If you _____, you will never get a good job.

    a. recover

    b. identify

    c. prevent

    d. drop out

15. He is _____ from a very serious disease.

    a. examining

    b. reducing

    c. conducting

    d. suffering

16. She is very _____. She is good at most sports.

    a. economic

    b. athletic

    c. intellectual

    d. characteristic

17. He went to the pharmacy to get the medicine that his doctor _____.

    a. suffered

    b. examined

    c. announced

    d. prescribed

18. She is on a very restricted _____. She can only eat vegetables.

    a. appearance   **c.** diet

    b. background   **d.** proof

19. They _____ to kill him if he didn't give them all of his money.

    a. poisoned   **c.** threatened

    b. contacted   **d.** survived

20. _____, women have made less money than men.

    a. In charge of   **c.** Historically

    b. On the basis of   **d.** Physically

21. She is in the hospital, recovering from a serious _____.

    a. cure   **c.** operation

    b. humanity   **d.** victim

22. I'm your friend. I will always _____ you.

    a. stand by   **c.** grow out of

    b. pick on   **d.** get rid of

23. I believe in freedom and _____ for all people.

    a. justice   **c.** background

    b. courage   **d.** mystery

24. Because of its beauty, that painting _____.

    a. burns out   **c.** brings up

    b. stands out   **d.** calls for

25. He won the competition _____ his illness.

    a. due to   **c.** despite

    b. on the basis of   **d.** at least

26. We gave her the job because of her strong _____ in international business.

    a. pattern   **c.** background

    b. instruction   **d.** challenge

27. Please stop making so much noise. I need to _____.

    a. concentrate   **c.** identify

    b. determine   **d.** prescribe

28. Fortunately, the patient _____ from the illness.

    a. suffered   **c.** intended

    b. progressed   **d.** recovered

29. She is the most _____ woman I know. She's not afraid of anything.

    a. beneficial   **c.** courageous

    b. fortunate   **d.** depressed

30. His work is _____, but not brilliant.

    a. acceptable   **c.** heavenly

    b. severe   **d.** evil

31. There are many _____ to getting a university education.

    a. complaints   **c.** traits

    b. concerns   **d.** advantages

32. I'm so sorry I woke you up. I didn't _____ it was so early.

    a. identify   **c.** intend

    b. realize   **d.** examine

33. Teenagers are usually very concerned about the opinions of their _____.

    a. experts   **c.** peers

    b. personalities   **d.** perfectionists

34. You were very _____ to survive the fire.

    a. evil   **c.** fortunate

    b. original   **d.** gifted

35. I wasn't _____ in the project. He did it by himself.

    a. fascinated   **c.** related

    b. involved   **d.** threatened

36. You don't need to bring any _____. We have all the tools we need to do the job.

    a. technique   **c.** equipment

    b. theory   **d.** challenge

See the Answer Key on page 256.

UNIT 4

GETTING EMOTIONAL

CHAPTER 10

Can You Translate an Emotion?

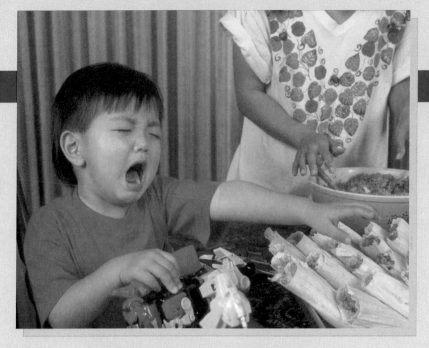

Children often have trouble controlling their emotions.

GETTING READY TO READ

 Talk with a partner or in a small group.

1. In general, is it easy or difficult for you to express your emotions? Which emotions do you often express? Which do you rarely express?

2. Who is the most emotional person you know? Describe him or her. Do you think that the fact that he or she is so emotional is positive or negative? Why?

B The **boldfaced** words below appear in the reading. Which words are new to you? Circle them. Then, work with a partner. Read the definitions of the words, and write one word under each picture.

anger = a strong feeling of wanting to hurt or criticize someone because he or she has done something bad to you or been unkind to you

cheerfulness = a happy, good feeling

disgust = a strong feeling of dislike and disapproval

grief = extreme sadness, especially because someone you love has died

guilt = a strong feeling of being ashamed and sad because you know or believe you have done something wrong

1. _____   2. _____   3. _____

4. _____   5. _____

READING

Read the text once without stopping.

Can You Translate an Emotion?

1   In the Northwest of Canada, there is a group of people called the Utkuhikhalingmiut ("Utku"). According to the anthropologist[1] Jean L. Briggs, author of the book *Never in Anger,* the Utku have no real word in their language for **anger**. And even more remarkable, they do not seem to ever get angry. The word that they use to describe the angry behavior of foreigners **translates** not as anger, but rather as "childishness."[2]

2   Similarly, the Ifaluk people of Micronesia seem to rarely get angry, and there is almost no murder in their culture. However, **in contrast** to the Utku, they talk about anger all the time and have many words to describe it. They consider anger to be evil—a demon,[3] in fact—and fear it.

3   The expression of **grief** and gratitude[4] is central to the Kaululi culture of Papua New Guinea. In contrast, people from the United States generally spend very little time talking about grief or gratitude. Research

continued

---

[1] an *anthropologist* = a person who studies people, their societies, beliefs, etc.

[2] *childishness* = behavior that is typical of a child

[3] a *demon* = an evil spirit

[4] *gratitude* = the feeling of wanting to express thanks for something kind that someone has done

on American males shows that they are **particularly** uncomfortable expressing either emotion.

4   What is going on here? Aren't we all human beings? Don't we all feel the same basic emotions? This is a topic that philosophers,[5] scientists, religious leaders, and anthropologists, among others, have been arguing about for centuries. Many researchers today believe that a limited number of emotions are **universal**. However, there is not complete agreement on which emotions humans **indeed** share. Fear and anger are almost always included; **guilt**, joy, **shame, disgust** and surprise are also considered by many to be universal. But then how can we explain the Utku and the Ifaluk?

5   Dr. Robert C. Solomon, professor of philosophy at the University of Texas at Austin, has argued that emotions are, at least in part, culture-specific. In one essay, he says that even among people from the same culture, it is difficult to get agreement on what an emotion is. For example, most anthropologists would not consider love to be an emotion, but if it is not an emotion, then what is it?

6   Another challenge is how to determine that two people are indeed feeling the same emotion. You can **observe** people's behavior, and ask them to describe their emotions, but it is impossible to directly observe what they are feeling. This becomes even more complex when you are trying to compare emotions across cultures.

7   We tend to **associate** certain behaviors with specific emotions, but of course our associations are based on what those behaviors mean in our own culture. For example, imagine you are a teacher with a Chinese student who has failed your class. Sadly, you learn that he **attempted** to hurt himself when he received his grade. If you are from the United States, you will probably describe his emotional state as depressed, for in U.S. culture, there is a belief that people who try to harm themselves are usually depressed. However, if you have some knowledge of Chinese culture, you might **recognize** your student's behavior as an expression of deep shame at having disgraced[6] his family.

8   Of course, this example is very simple—it does not mean that the Chinese do not ever experience depression, or that people from the United States do not feel shame. However, can someone from a culture that does not place the same value on family **honor** really understand this deep feeling of disgrace? In other words, is Chinese shame and American shame really the same emotion?

continued

------

[5] a *philosopher* = a person who studies or teaches about the world, life, death, etc.

[6] *disgrace* = to do something so bad that people lose respect for you

9   Another reason to believe that not all emotions are universal is the fact that different languages characterize emotions in different ways. For instance, in the ancient Indian languages of Sanskrit and Bengali, emotions are described as being either *sattva* (lightness), *rajas* (movement), or *tamas* (heaviness). Interestingly, two of the examples of *sattva*—**cheerfulness** and nobility[7]—are not generally considered to be emotions in English. Is this just a language difference? Or does it **reveal** that people across cultures do not share a similar emotional experience?

10   The mystery of whether emotions are universal or culturally specific is one that most likely will never be solved. That probably contributes to our fascination with the subject.

---

[7] *nobility* = the quality of being morally good or generous in a way that should be admired

Comprehension Check

Read these sentences. Circle T (true), F (false) or ? (can't determine the answer from the reading). If you circle F, change the sentence to make it true. Check your answers with a classmate. If your answers are different, look back at the reading.

1. All languages have words for the most basic human emotions.   T   F   ?

2. In the Utku culture, people who express anger are considered childish.   T   F   ?

3. The basic human emotions are universal, not culture-specific.   T   F   ?

4. Because we cannot know exactly what other people are feeling, we observe their behavior and then try to guess what they are feeling.   T   F   ?

5. The shame that an American feels is different from the shame that a Chinese person feels.   T   F   ?

6. The word *sattva* means cheerfulness.   T   F   ?

EXPLORING VOCABULARY

Thinking about the Vocabulary

Guessing Strategy

You learned in the **Guessing Strategy** for Chapter 4 that to avoid repeating words, writers often use synonyms. They also use words that have similar meanings, but are different word forms. Look at the example.

> Many researchers today believe that a limited number of emotions are **universal**. However, there is not complete agreement on which emotions humans indeed share.

Based on the context, you can guess that the words *universal* and *share* have a similar meaning, even though *universal* is an adjective and *share* is a verb.

Try It!

Read the sentences, and write the word or words that are similar in meaning to the **boldfaced** target word.

> His emotions are not hidden from anybody. He **reveals** whatever he is feeling

Reveals is similar in meaning to _____

Look at the target words and phrases. Which ones are new to you? Circle them here and in the reading. Then read "Can You Translate an Emotion?" again. Look at the context of each new word and phrase. Can you guess the meaning? Use the Guessing Strategy where possible.

Target Words and Phrases

anger (1)	universal (4)	disgust (4)	recognize (7)
translates (1)	indeed (4)	observe (6)	honor (8)
in contrast (2)	guilt (4)	associate (7)	cheerfulness (9)
grief (3)	shame (4)	attempted (7)	reveal (9)
particularly (3)			

Using the Vocabulary

These sentences are **about the reading**. Complete them with the words and phrases in the box. Circle the words or phrases in the sentences that help you understand the meanings of the target words.

associate	attempted	honor	in contrast	indeed	observe
particularly	recognize	reveal	shame	translate	universal

1. Are human emotions culturally specific, or are they _____?

2. Experts in many fields have _____ to answer this question for years, but we still don't know the answer.

3. Answering the question is _____ difficult because we cannot "see" an emotion. We cannot _____ someone's feelings directly.

4. How do we know what others are feeling? We usually look at their behavior, and then _____ it with an emotion. In other words, we believe that actions _____, or show, a person's true feelings.

5. However, the same behavior in one culture might mean something different in another. Therefore, it is not always easy to _____ which emotions individuals from another country are expressing through their behavior.

6. For example, Americans think that people who deliberately try to hurt themselves are depressed. _____, in Chinese culture, such behavior is often associated with _____ and guilt.

7. Because the Chinese believe that the reputation and _____ of a family are very important, a Chinese student who brings shame to his family by getting poor grades might consider harming himself.

8. Another problem is that it is not always easy to _____ the words of emotion from one language to another. _____, in the Utku culture in Northwest Canada, there appears to be no word at all for *anger*.

DEVELOPING READING SKILLS

Understanding Inference

Answer these questions in your own words. The answers are not written directly in the reading. You will need to infer them. There might be more than one correct way to answer each question.

1. In paragraph 3, the reading says that "males in the United States . . . are particularly uncomfortable expressing either emotion." From this sentence, what can you infer about *females* in the United States?

   _____

   _____

2. How do you think Utku parents react when their young children behave in an angry way? Be specific.

   _____

   _____

3. How do you think Ifaluk parents react when their young children behave in an angry way? Be specific.

   _____

   _____

Paraphrasing

When you **paraphrase** a sentence, you use different words. However, you do not change the meaning of the original sentence. Look at the paraphrase of this sentence from the reading.

> *Original sentence:* Grief and gratitude are central to the Kaululi culture of Papua New Guinea.

> *Paraphrase:* For the Kaululi people who live in Papua New Guinea, grief and gratitude are very important emotions.

Notice that you do not have to change *all* of the words when you paraphrase.

One sentence in each set paraphrases the sentence from the reading. Circle the correct answer.

1. Many researchers today believe that a limited number of emotions are universal.

   a. A lot of experts agree that most people experience at least a few of the same emotions, regardless of which country they come from.

   b. People who study human emotions think that all human beings share the same emotions.

2. However, there is not complete agreement on which emotions humans indeed share.

   a. But the emotions noted by one group of experts are completely different from those of another group of experts.

   b. But not all experts agree on which feelings are indeed universal.

3. This becomes even more complex when you are trying to compare emotions across cultures.

   a. It is particularly difficult to describe the emotions of two people who come from different cultures.

   b. It is not easy to compare people who come from different parts of the world.

EXPANDING VOCABULARY

Using the Vocabulary in New Contexts

These sentences use the target words and phrases **in new contexts.** Complete them with the words and phrases in the box.

associate	attempt	honor	in contrast	indeed	observe
particularly	recognize	reveal	shame	translate	universal

1. It is an _____ to be seated next to the President.

2. I'd rather not go to that movie. I'm not _____ interested in war films.

3. If you eat something that makes you sick, you will always _____ that food with your illness.

4. Please wear a red coat so that I will _____ you in the crowd.

5. You are so courageous! I would be afraid to even _____ to climb that mountain!

6. This letter is too complex for me to _____. My Spanish is not that good.

7. There are many feelings that may vary among cultures, but the need for love is probably _____.

8. The doctor is almost certain that the patient has recovered, but he still wants to _____ her for 24 hours.

9. *In fact* and _____ have the same meaning.

10. The competition lasts for a week. They will _____ the winner on the last day.

11. Tom felt terrible about the car accident. He felt both guilt and _____ that the little girl was hurt.

12. That drug can be harmful. This drug, _____, is harmless.

Word Families

Study the chart. Look at the adjective forms of the target words. Then, complete the sentences with words from the chart. Make sure you use the correct word forms. Be careful; you will not use all the words.

Noun: Names the emotion	Adjective: Describes the way someone feels	Adjective: Describes what/who causes the feeling
Example: *His **shame** at what he had done bothered him for the rest of his life.*	Example: *You made her cry. You should be **ashamed** of yourself!*	Example: *The way you treated her was **shameful**.*
anger	angry	
shame	ashamed	shameful
cheerfulness	cheerful	cheerful or cheery
disgust	disgusted	disgusting
guilt	guilty	

1. This soup smells _____. I can't eat it!

2. After he stole the money, he felt _____, so he decided to give it back.

3. Her shame kept her quiet her entire life. She never revealed her _____ secret to anyone.

4. It's difficult to feel depressed around her because she's always so _____.

5. Some people shout and throw things when they are _____.

6. After I found a hair in my food, I was so _____ that I couldn't eat.

7. The mother felt _____ when her son was sent home from school for behaving badly in class.

Studying Word Grammar

You learned in Unit 3 that transitive verbs always have a direct object. Often, the direct object is a noun or pronoun. Look at the sentence using the transitive verb **recognize**.

                      pronoun   *pronoun*
She didn't **recognize** *me*, but I **recognized** *her*.

In some cases, the direct object is not a noun or pronoun. Look at the transitive verbs **attempt** and **observe**.

    We all **attempted** *to help* her, but unfortunately we couldn't.

In the example above, *attempt* is followed by an **infinitive**: *to* + verb.

    The doctor **observed** *that the patient was able to move his left leg.*

In the example above, *observe* is followed by a full **clause**: *that* + subject + verb. Different verbs have different patterns. In order to use a verb correctly, you need to learn the pattern(s) for that particular verb. If you are not sure, look in your dictionary.

A Look at the patterns in the box above for the verbs *recognize, attempt,* and *observe.* Then, read the sentences, and put a check (✓) next to those that are correct and an X next to those that are incorrect.

_____ 1. When the police showed the victim several photographs, she recognized her attacker immediately.

_____ 2. The victim attempted identify her attacker, but she couldn't.

_____ 3. The police observed the man to behave in a strange way.

_____ 4. The researchers observed that all of the mice in the experiment had the same reaction to the chemical.

_____ 5. The police attempted to catch the man with the gun, but he escaped.

_____ 6. He tried to get away, but someone recognized him and called the police.

B Answer these questions in complete sentences. Use the **boldfaced** verbs. Make sure you use the correct patterns.

1. Describe a time when you **attempted** to do something difficult, but failed.

_____

_____

_____

2. Choose a culture other than your own that you are familiar with. What differences have you **observed** between the two cultures?

_____

_____

_____

3. What would you do if you **recognized** your favorite actor on the street?

_____

_____

_____

PUTTING IT ALL TOGETHER

Discussion

Share your ideas in a small group. As you talk, try to use the vocabulary below. Each time someone uses a target word or phrase, put a check (✓) next to it.

anger/angry	attempt	disgust/disgusted/disgusting
grief	guilt/guilty	honor
in contrast	indeed	observe
particularly	reveal	shame/ashamed/shameful

1. Choose one of the emotions from the list above, and tell your group about a time when you or someone you know felt that way. Include details (for example, *who, what, where, when,* and *how*) to make your story come alive for your classmates.
2. Some people think that it is healthy to express emotions openly. Other people believe that it is best to control their emotions and not reveal them to others. What are the advantages and disadvantages of each approach?

Writing

Choose one or both of the Discussion questions above to write about. When you write, use at least five of the target words from the chapter. Underline the target words in your paper.

CHAPTER 11

Japanese Trying Service with a Smile

"I wonder what their secret is?"

GETTING READY TO READ

 First, complete the chart. Then, compare your answers with a partner.

When you are a customer in a restaurant, clothing store, or gas station, what do you expect from the people working there? Write 1 for very important, 2 for somewhat important, and 3 for not important.

	Friendliness and a smile	Fast service	High-quality product	Knowledge of the product or service
Restaurant				
Clothing store				
Gas station				

B The **boldfaced** words and phrases in the paragraph below appear in the reading. Which words are new to you? Circle them. Then, work with a partner. Read this paragraph introducing the topic of the reading, and match the words with their definitions.

In Japan, some businesses are sending workers to "smile schools." The teachers at these schools attempt to get students to relax the **muscles** of their faces, smile, and even laugh **out loud**—things the naturally **reserved** Japanese rarely do. In a competitive economy, managers of service companies hope that by having their employees **greet** customers with a friendly **facial expression**, sales will increase.

Word	Definition
_____ 1. muscles	a. in a way that people can hear your voice
_____ 2. out loud	b. unwilling to express your emotions or talk about your problems
_____ 3. reserved	c. a look on someone's face that shows what he or she is thinking or feeling
_____ 4. greet	d. say hello to or welcome someone
_____ 5. facial expression	e. the pieces of flesh inside your body that join bones together and make your body move

READING

Read the text once without stopping.

Japanese Trying Service with a Smile

1   It is Wednesday night, and Hiroshi Ieyoshi and 36 other gas station attendants[1] are involved in some difficult after-hours training. They are learning how to smile. Or rather, trying to learn. "Relax the **muscle** under your nose," teacher Akio Emi instructs them. "Relax your tongue. Put your hands on your stomach and laugh **out loud**, feeling the 'poisons' escape." Even if you are feeling depressed, Emi says, give the customers an **artificial** smile and your emotions are likely to follow. "In this recession,[2] customers are getting **choosy** about their gas stations, so you have to think positively," Emi says.

continued

---

[1] an *attendant* = someone whose job is to help people in a public place
[2] a *recession* = a period of time when there is less business activity or trade than usual

2   All this advice is not making it any easier for Ieyoshi, who just can not pretend. ``It's easy to say you should smile at the customers," the 33-year-old says after the 90-minute class. ``But to be honest, it all depends on how I feel at the moment."

3   Getting employees to smile at work has become serious business in Japan. Many businesses are sending workers to "smile schools," which teach techniques such as biting on a chopstick.[3] They hope that their sales will rise along with employees' lips.

4   This is a particularly big change for Japan, where smiling at strangers—even if they are customers—has always been, well, **frowned upon**. Employees **greet** customers with a simple *Irasshaimase*— "Welcome"—but usually do not give a friendly smile, stop to talk, or even offer an informal "How are you?" or "Have a nice day."

5   Japanese culture calls for controlling both positive and negative emotions—whether they are happy, sad, or angry—to keep the *wa,* or group **harmony**. In this formal society, families rarely touch, hug, or kiss in public.

6   "It's so deep in our Japanese **consciousness** that it's not **proper** to move the face or body too much," explains Hiroto Murasawa, who works at the Pola Research **Institute** of Beauty and Culture in Tokyo. Until the twentieth century, he says, some Japanese women shaved their **eyebrows** and made their teeth black to hide their natural **facial expressions**. Many Japanese women still hide their mouths behind a hand when they speak or laugh. For men, too, hiding emotion has been considered a **virtue**. Of course, the Japanese are not without **humor**. It is just that their expressions are so much more **reserved** than those of people from most other countries, including Asian neighbors such as South Korea and China, says Murasawa.

7   According to Yoshihiko Kadokawa, the author of the book *Power of a Laughing Face* and president of his own company, the Smile Amenity[4] Institute, everybody benefits when employees smile. Not only do customers buy more when they get a warm feeling from workers, but employees feel better about their work and the number of absences goes down.

8   A Japanese photographer in one of Kadokawa's classes thinks that the course should be taught to Japanese wives. "American wives smile at their husbands. Japanese wives never do," he complains. Assistant manager Kentaro Ito, 29, is excited about the positive results he has seen at his store since starting the once-a-week classes several weeks ago.

continued

---

[3] *chopsticks* = a pair of thin sticks used for eating food, especially by people in Asia
[4] an *amenity* = something in a place that makes living there enjoyable and pleasant

9   For instructor Emi, the group who has the most trouble relaxing is young men in their twenties and thirties. Those at the class for gas station attendants are having a hard time understanding the practice techniques Emi has invented, such as "underwater training," in which students put their faces in water and then breathe out while laughing.

10   Of course, smile too much and the customer might think you are crazy. Kutaro Matsunaga, an unusually cheerful gas station attendant wearing a checked[5] suit and gold vest,[6] says his customers sometimes look at him strangely when he talks to them in his usual cheerful way. "They think I'm nuts[7]—I can sense that when I talk to them. But my name means 'happy man,' and I always want to make my customers happy."

11   The class was helpful, several of the attendants say. Some, however, are still nervous about whether they can do it. Komorita Manabu, 26, says he hopes to **make up for** not smiling by greeting customers "with a big, clear and loud voice" as they drive into the station, while still providing all the usual services such as cleaning the windshield[8] and guiding the car in and out of traffic.

12   It is still difficult for Ieyoshi. "If you don't feel open to strangers, you don't smile," he says. "Maybe I'm living in a closed, hard shell,[9] but the Japanese character is not to express your emotions."

---

[5] *checked* = having a regular pattern of different-colored squares

[6] *vest* = a piece of clothing without sleeves that has buttons down the front, worn over a shirt

[7] *nuts* = crazy

[8] a *windshield* = the large window at the front of a car

[9] *living in a shell* = having an attitude that hides emotions and feelings

Comprehension Check

Read these sentences. Circle T (true) or F (false). If you circle F, change the sentence to make it true. Check your answers with a classmate. If your answers are different, look back at the reading.

1. Traditionally, the Japanese were taught not to reveal their emotions through their facial expressions.   T   F

2. The Japanese do not appreciate humor.   T   F

3. Traditionally, the Japanese have tended to be more reserved than people from other Asian countries.   T   F

4. The purpose of "smile schools" is to help students feel less depressed about their economic problems.   T   F

5. Young Japanese men find it particularly difficult to relax.   T   F

6. In Japan, gas station attendants typically perform services   T   F
   for their customers, including helping them to enter and exit
   the station.

EXPLORING VOCABULARY

Thinking about the Vocabulary

Guessing Strategy

Look carefully at an unfamiliar word. Does it look like another word you already know? If so, it might be a form of that word. Look at the example from the reading.

> Until the twentieth century, he notes, some Japanese women shaved their eyebrows and made their teeth black to hide their natural **facial expressions**.

Facial is the adjective form of the noun *face*. *Expression* is the noun form of the verb *express*. A facial expression is a look on a person's face that shows what that person is thinking or feeling.

Try It!

Read the sentences and answer the questions.

> In some cultures, expressing emotions is accepted. In other cultures, expressing emotion is **frowned upon**.

1. What word is similar to **frowned**? _____

2. What does that word mean? _____

3. What does **frowned upon** mean? _____

Look at the target words and phrases. Which ones are new to you? Circle them here and in the reading. Then read "Japanese Trying Service with a Smile" again. Look at the context of each new word and phrase. Can you guess the meaning? Use the Guessing Strategy where possible.

Target Words and Phrases

muscle (1)	**frowned upon** (4)	**proper** (6)	**virtue** (6)
out loud (1)	**greet** (4)	**institute** (6)	**humor** (6)
artificial (1)	**harmony** (5)	**eyebrows** (6)	**reserved** (6)
choosy (1)	**consciousness** (6)	**facial expressions** (6)	**make up for** (11)

Using the Vocabulary

These sentences are **about the reading**. Complete them with the words and phrases in the box. Circle the words or phrases in the sentences that help you understand the meanings of the target words.

artificial	choosy	consciousness	eyebrows	frowned upon	harmony
humor	institute	make up for	proper	virtue	

1. In traditional Japanese culture, people were taught that it was correct to hide their feelings from others. It was not considered _____ to reveal one's emotions.

2. In fact, people believed that hiding their emotions was a moral thing to do. They considered it a _____.

3. Historically, some Japanese women even shaved their _____ so that their facial expressions would not reveal their emotions.

4. In Japan, smiling at strangers is not common, or even acceptable. In fact, it is _____.

5. Most Japanese are emotionally reserved. This is a part of the Japanese _____. It involves their deepest feelings and beliefs.

6. Since group needs are seen as more important than individual needs in Japan, group _____ is very important. Individuals control or hide their emotions to avoid upsetting other group members.

7. However, although Japanese people are more reserved than people from many other countries, they do enjoy _____. They just don't tend to smile at strangers or laugh out loud very often.

8. Due to a slow economy in Japan, customers are more _____ about where they shop, eat, and buy gas. As a result, to attract more customers, some companies are sending their employees to "smile schools."

9. There is a smile school in Japan. This _____ was developed by a man who believes that customers buy more when employees smile at them.

10. Some people do not feel comfortable making _____ smiles and pretending they are happy.

11. The employees who do not feel comfortable smiling hope that they can _____ it by giving customers excellent service.

DEVELOPING READING SKILLS

Scanning

Scan the reading and find the six techniques for learning how to smile.

1. <u>Relax the muscle under your nose.</u>
2. _____
3. _____
4. _____
5. _____
6. _____

Understanding Reference Words

A **reference word** is a word that takes the place of a noun or noun phrase. Pronouns (such as *he, she, it,* and *them*) are reference words. A reference word usually comes after a noun or noun phrase and refers back to it. The words *this, that, these, those, that, which, who,* and *whom* are also reference words.

What do the boldfaced reference words mean in these sentences? Look back at the reading, and circle the correct answers. The number in parentheses is the paragraph number where the sentence appears.

1. "Relax the muscle under **your** nose," teacher Akio Emi instructs **them**." (1)

   In this sentence, *your* refers to

   a. employers.   **b.** readers.   **c.** employees.

   Them refers to

   a. employers.   **b.** readers.   **c.** employees.

2. Many retail and service businesses are sending workers to "smile schools," **which** teach techniques such as biting on a chopstick. **They** hope that sales will rise along with employees' lips. (3)

   In these sentences, *which* refers to

   a. retail and service   **b.** techniques.   **c.** smile schools.
   businesses.

   They refers to

   a. retail and service   **b.** workers.   **c.** smile schools.
   businesses.

3. It's just that their expressions are so much more reserved than **those** of people from most other countries. (6)

In this sentence, *those* refers to

a. people from other countries.   b. the Japanese.   c. the expressions.

4. "They think I'm nuts—I can sense **that** when I talk to them." (10)

In this sentence *that* refers to

a. what customers think.   b. what he thinks.   c. what the employees think.

EXPANDING VOCABULARY

Using the Vocabulary in New Contexts

These sentences use the target words and phrases **in new contexts.**
Complete them with the words and phrases in the box.

artificial	choosy	consciousness	eyebrows	frowned upon	harmony
humor	institutes	make up for	proper	virtue	

1. Your behavior was really insensitive. However, you can _____ it by taking me out to dinner.

2. When you travel, it is important to know which behaviors are _____ in that culture. That way, you will know how to behave politely.

3. My uncle has very thick _____ and a big moustache.

4. In some traditional cultures, a woman going out alone at night is still _____.

5. Please don't fight. We should all be able to live together in peace and _____.

6. In the American _____, it is considered important to be independent.

7. I don't like food with _____ ingredients. I like to eat healthy, natural food.

8. If you want to survive in this economy, you can't be _____ about which job you take. You should feel fortunate to have a job!

9. There are many language _____ where you can learn English.

10. He has a great sense of _____. He always makes me laugh.

11. Most people would probably agree that honesty is a _____.

Word Families

Some adjectives are formed by adding –*y* to the end of a word. Look at the example.

> My daughter is only three years old, but she is already very **choosy**. For example, she won't let me choose her clothes. She likes to choose her own.

Sometimes, the meaning of the adjective will be very close to the meaning of the original word, but in some cases, you will need to use the context to guess what the adjective means. Notice that the spelling sometimes changes when you add –*y*.

Complete the sentences with the adjectives below.

airy   juicy   picky   smelly   watery

1. No one likes to invite her for dinner because she's such a

    _____ eater. It's impossible to remember all the types of food

    that she won't eat.

2. These oranges are delicious! They are so sweet and _____.

3. I can't drink this coffee. It's too _____. I like stronger coffee.

4. This room is so bright and _____. And look at the beautiful

    view!

5. Some people do not like strong cheese. They think that it is too

    _____.

Studying Phrasal Verbs

The phrasal verb **make up for** means "to make a bad situation seem better, by providing something nice." There are several phrasal verbs that are formed with the verb *make* and the particle *up*. Each one has a different meaning.

Read the definitions for *make up* and the sentences that follow. Write the letter of the meaning next to each sentence.

a. prepare or arrange something by putting things together

b. work or study at times when you do not usually work, so that you do all the work that you should have done at an earlier time

c. become friendly again with someone after you have had an argument

d. invent a story, explanation, etc.

_____ 1. I missed the exam because I was sick. Can I **make** it **up**?

_____ 2. That isn't a true story. He **made** it **up**.

_____ 3. My husband and I had a fight last week, but yesterday we **made up**.

_____ 4. I'll **make up** a list of things we need for the party, and then we can go shopping.

PUTTING IT ALL TOGETHER

Discussion

Share your ideas in a small group. As you talk, try to use the vocabulary below each question. Each time someone uses a target word or phrase, put a check (✓) next to it.

1. Describe the best or worst service that you've ever received. Consider service in the following places: a hotel; a restaurant; a gas station; a clothing store; the post office; a government office (for example, the place where you get your driver's license); a hair salon.

   choosy   greet   make up for   proper   reserved

2. The reading says that business managers in Japan hope that sales will increase if their employees smile more. The president of the Smile Amenity Institute, Yoshihiko Kadokawa, claims that customers buy more when workers are friendly. At the same time, workers enjoy their work more and tend to be absent less. Do you agree with this point of view? Do you think that it's possible to "teach" someone how to be friendly and smile more? Explain your answers.

facial expression	frowned upon	greet	harmony	humor
laugh out loud	make up for	proper	reserved	virtue

Writing

Complete one or both of these writing topics. When you write, use at least five of the target words from the chapter. Underline the target words in your paper.

1. Write an essay. Describe the qualities that a person who works in a service position (for example, as a waiter, gas station attendant, or salesperson in a clothing store) should have.

2. Think about (or invent) a time when you received very bad service. Write a letter of complaint to the management.

CHAPTER 12

Road Rage

Angry drivers can be dangerous.

GETTING READY TO READ

 How aggressive is your driving? Answer the questions shown in the chart. (If you don't drive, choose someone you know and answer based on what you have observed of that person's driving.) First, complete the chart alone. Then, compare your answers in a small group.

How often do you . . .	Very often	Sometimes	Rarely	Never
drive faster than the speed limit?				
not stop at a red light?				
not stop at a stop sign?				
shout or gesture angrily at other drivers?				
sound your horn or flash your lights to make a slower driver get out of the way?				

B The **boldfaced** words below all appear in the reading. **Which words are new to you? Circle them.** Then, **work with a partner. Read the definitions of the words, and complete the sentences below the pictures with the words.**

gesture = tell what you mean or feel by moving your arms, hands, or head

pregnant = having an unborn baby growing in your body

pull in front of = move a car, truck, etc., in front of someone or something

slammed = hit someone, something, or a part of one's body against a surface, quickly and with a lot of force

witness = someone who sees an accident or crime and can describe it

1. She is eight months _____.

2. She _____ the door in his face.

3. The police officer is asking the _____ what happened.

4. Drivers often _____ when they are angry.

5. You should be careful when you _____ another car.

READING

Read the text once without stopping.

Road Rage

1   The women were driving their cars just outside the U. S. city of Cincinnati, Ohio. Rene Andrews, 29, was six-months **pregnant** with her first child. Tracie Alfieri, 23, was the mother of two. Suddenly, Andrews **pulled in front of** Alfieri. Alfieri **gestured** angrily at Andrews, sped up, and drove her Pontiac past and in front of Andrews' Volkswagen, prosecutors[1] say. Alfieri, police say, then **slammed** on the brakes.[2] Andrews swerved[3] to the right and crashed into a truck parked on the side of the road. She was seriously **injured**—and she lost her unborn child.

2   Alfieri's lawyer, Timothy Schneider, says she stepped on the brakes because there was traffic ahead. However, the court found Alfieri guilty of aggravated vehicular homicide[4] and aggravated vehicular assault.[5] The judge ordered her to spend 18 months in prison. After six months, she was allowed to leave prison to take care of a sick daughter.

3   The prosecutor of the case says his office has dealt with plenty of cases involving aggressive driving, but none that ended as violently as this one. "Alfieri's conduct[6] was so aggravated . . . it was so bad, that a **witness** to it followed her all the way to work to get her license number," prosecutor Joseph Deters says.

4   Two years after the accident in November 1996, Andrews was still recovering. She and her husband have nearly $200,000 in medical bills. "She's hoping that she can still have children, but she doesn't know," Robin Levine, Andrews' lawyer says.

5   The term "road rage" has no exact **legal** definition, but it is commonly used when "a driver or passenger attempts to kill, injure, or intimidate[7] a

continued

---

1 a *prosecutor* = a lawyer who is trying to prove in a court of law that someone is guilty of a crime

2 *brakes* = equipment that makes a vehicle (car, truck, etc.) go more slowly or stop

3 *swerve* = turn suddenly and dangerously while driving

4 *aggravated vehicular homicide* = the crime of killing someone with a car because you were driving in a dangerous way

5 *aggravated vehicular assault* = the crime of attacking someone with a car

6 *conduct* = the way someone behaves

7 *intimidate* = make someone afraid, often by using threats, so that she or he does what you want

pedestrian[8] or another driver or passenger or to **damage** their **vehicle** in a traffic **incident**," (*Canadian Medical Association Journal*, October 1, 2002). In recent years, English-language newspapers around the world have been publishing many stories on **sensational** cases like that of Andrews and Alfieri, and there has been a lot written about the cause of this "new" aggression on the roads. The explanations **range** from an increase in traffic to the anxiety people feel due to rapid technological change.

6   However, some researchers doubt that this is actually a "new" problem. They believe that the recent attention given to road rage is the result of the media's desire to sell more papers or increase their number of viewers. These researchers **accuse** the media of inventing the term "road rage" to sensationalize what is not a societal problem, but rather a personal **tragedy** affecting a very limited number of individuals.

7   It is difficult to determine whether or not aggressive driving is increasing. Because there is no legal definition of road rage, incidents are reported differently from town to town. Still, the U.S. Department of Transportation **calculates** that two-thirds of traffic deaths in the United States are at least partly caused by aggressive driving. In a 2002 Canadian study, 88 percent of drivers surveyed admitted to aggressive driving—such as speeding or going through yellow lights—in the previous year, an increase of 3 percent over the year before. And a recent survey done for Axa Direct, a British **insurance** company, showed that three out of every four drivers or passengers had experienced some form of road rage. However, it is important to note that only 1 percent reported having actually experienced a physical attack.

8   One thing that all researchers would likely agree on, however, is that the best way to deal with road rage is to prevent it from ever happening. In the United States, researchers are conducting tests with a simple machine called "the Flash" to see if it will help reduce incidents of aggressive driving. Drivers participating in the experiment will get a green light to put in their vehicle's back windows, and a button to **flash** it on and off. One flash means "Please," as in "Please let me get in front of you," two flashes means "Thank you," and three flashes means "I am sorry." Before drivers in an area start using "The Flash," there will be advertisements to educate the public about its use. The hope is that if drivers can communicate even just these few basic ideas and feelings to each other, there will be less of a tendency for them to react to each other with rage.

---

[8] a *pedestrian* = someone who is walking instead of driving a car or riding a bicycle

Comprehension Check

Read these sentences. Circle T (true) or F (false). If you circle F, change the sentence to make it true. Check your answers with a classmate. If your answers are different, look back at the reading.

1. Road rage is a crime in the United States, Canada, and   T   F
   Britain.

2. All aggressive drivers have been involved in accidents.   T   F

3. It is not clear whether incidents of road rage have been   T   F
   increasing in recent years.

4. Researchers studying road rage say that it is due to a   T   F
   variety of causes.

5. Studies show that aggressive driving is not very common.   T   F

6. The use of "the Flash" has become very popular among   T   F
   drivers in the United States.

EXPLORING VOCABULARY

Thinking about the Vocabulary

Guessing Strategy

You can sometimes guess the meaning of a word or phrase by imagining the scene that it describes. Look at the example, and form a picture in your mind for the **boldfaced** words and phrases.

> Two cars were traveling next to each other on a large highway. Suddenly, one car **pulled in front of** the other. The driver of the second car had to **slam** on the brakes to avoid hitting the first car.

To check your "picture," ask yourself questions. For example: *What can one car suddenly do to another car that is traveling next to it? What can a driver do to avoid hitting another car?*

Try It!

Read the sentence, and write a definition of the **boldfaced** target word.

> The car in front of me was moving too slowly, so I **flashed** my lights to signal that I wanted to pass.

Flash means _____

Look at the target words and phrases. Which ones are new to you? Circle them here and in the reading. Then read "Road Rage" again. Look at the context of each new word and phrase. Can you guess the meaning? Use the Guessing Strategy where possible.

Target Words and Phrases

rage (title)	injured (1)	incident (5)	tragedy (6)
pregnant (1)	witness (3)	sensational (5)	calculates (7)
pulled in front of (1)	legal (5)	range (5)	insurance (7)
gestured (1)	damage (5)	accuse (6)	flash (8)
slammed (1)	vehicle (5)		

Using the Vocabulary

These sentences are **about the reading**. What is the meaning of each **boldfaced** word or phrase? Circle a, b, or c. Then circle the words or phrases in the sentences that help you understand the meanings of the target words.

1. Road **rage** is an expression that is used to describe the behavior of some drivers who become very, very mad at another driver. *Rage* means

   a. guilt. **b.** anger. **c.** disrespect.

2. Rene Andrews was pregnant when she was seriously **injured** in a road rage incident. As a result, she lost her baby. *Injured* means

   a. angry. **b.** hurt. **c.** in trouble.

3. Tracy Alfieri is the name of the other driver involved in the **incident** that resulted in the death of Rene Andrews' baby. An *incident* is something

   a. that happens more than one time. **b.** that happens by mistake. **c.** unusual, serious, or violent that happens.

4. The police **accused** Alfieri of slamming on her brakes and causing Andrews' accident. When you *accuse* someone of doing something, you

   a. say that the person did something wrong. **b.** are guilty. **c.** send the person to prison.

5. What happened to Alfieri and Andrews was a terrible **tragedy**. Their lives will never be the same again. A *tragedy* is

   a. an extremely sad event. **b.** a story that is not true. **c.** extreme anger.

6. The incident involving Alfieri and Andrews was so **sensational** that it was written about in many newspapers. Something that is *sensational* is

   a. intended to shock or excite people.　　**b.** not particularly interesting.　　**c.** sad and depressing.

7. The court decided that Alfieri had used her **vehicle** as a weapon to injure Andrews. It is not **legal** to use your car in that way. That is why Alfieri was sent to prison. Examples of *vehicles* include

   a. guns and knives.　　**b.** cars and trucks.　　**c.** injuring and killing.

   Legal means

   a. morally wrong.　　**b.** a good idea.　　**c.** allowed by law.

8. The term *road rage* is not only used to describe incidents in which one driver injures another. It is also used when one driver **damages** another driver's car. *Damage* means to

   a. completely destroy.　　**b.** cause harm to.　　**c.** get into an accident.

9. It is difficult to **calculate** exactly how many traffic accidents are due to road rage, because there is no legal definition of road rage. When you *calculate* something, you

   a. reduce it a little.　　**b.** deal with it.　　**c.** measure it using numbers.

10. The definition of road rage includes acts that **range** from scratching someone's car to causing someone's death. *Range* means

    a. result in.　　**b.** be serious.　　**c.** vary.

11. **Insurance** companies want to find out more about the connection between aggressive driving and traffic accidents. That's because they pay for damages or injuries their clients cause while they are driving. Automobile *insurance* companies

    a. pay for the damage if their client gets in an accident.　　**b.** help their clients avoid traffic accidents.　　**c.** borrow money if their clients get into an accident.

12. Aggressive drivers typically **flash** their lights at slower drivers to make them get out of the way. When you *flash* your lights, you

    a. keep them on all day.　　**b.** turn them on when it gets dark.　　**c.** turn them on and then immediately off.

DEVELOPING READING SKILLS

Understanding Inference

Answer these questions in your own words. The answers are not written directly in the reading. You will need to infer them.

1. Do you think that Tracy Alfieri and Renee Andrews knew each other before the incident occurred? Explain why you think that way.

   _____

   _____

   _____

2. Did Alfieri stop her car when Andrews' car went off the road? Explain.

   _____

   _____

   _____

3. What specifically will the advertisements about "the Flash" teach the public?

   _____

   _____

   _____

Paraphrasing

Remember that when you paraphrase what someone else has written, you change the structure of the sentence and some of the words, but you do not change the meaning of the original sentence. If the original sentence is long or complex, you might need more than one sentence to paraphrase it.

 One sentence in each set paraphrases the sentence from the reading. Circle the correct answer.

1. However, some researchers doubt that road rage is actually a "new" problem.

   a. But there are researchers who believe that road rage has existed for a long time.

   b. But some researchers don't believe that road rage exists.

2. They believe that the recent attention given to road rage is the result of the media's desire to sell more papers or increase their number of viewers.

   a. Some researchers think that people in the media want more people to buy their newspapers or watch their television shows. That is the only reason they focus so much on road rage.

   b. Some people in the media think that if they write about road rage a lot, the number of road rage incidents will increase. When that happens, their newspapers or TV stations will make more money.

3. In a 2002 Canadian study, 88 percent of drivers surveyed admitted to aggressive driving . . . an increase of 3 percent over the previous year.

   a. In the year 2002, 88 percent of Canadian drivers told researchers that they had driven aggressively. In the previous year, the percentage of aggressive drivers was 3 percent higher.

   b. In the year 2001, in one survey of drivers in Canada, 85 percent said that they had driven aggressively during that year. In the same survey the following year, that figure had climbed to 88 percent.

B Paraphrase these sentences from the reading. The numbers in parentheses are the paragraphs that the sentences come from.

1. It is difficult to determine whether or not aggressive driving is increasing. (7)

   _____

2. Still, the U.S. Department of Transportation calculates that two-thirds of traffic deaths in the United States are at least partly caused by aggressive driving. (7)

   _____

   _____

EXPANDING VOCABULARY

Using the Vocabulary in New Contexts

These sentences use the target words and phrases **in new contexts**. Complete them with the words and phrases in the box.

accuse	calculate	damaged	flashed	incident	injured
insurance	legal	rage	range	sensational	tragedy
vehicle					

1. If you want _____ advice, you should go to a lawyer.

2. Shakespeare's *Romeo and Juliet* is a _____. Both characters die at the end.

3. He was in a _____ because he discovered that someone had stolen his computer.

4. When I was in the hospital, my health _____ paid for everything.

5. I worked a lot of extra hours last week. I need to _____ what my paycheck will be.

6. There was an unfortunate _____ at the store where I work last night. Two employees started fighting, and the police had to come to separate them.

7. Without proof, you can't _____ him of stealing your wallet.

8. He _____ a muscle in his shoulder, so he can't play in the game tonight.

9. You need a special license to drive a _____ with more than four wheels.

10. He's a doctor, but his interests _____ from medical research to rap music.

11. I'm sorry I _____ your stereo. Is there anything I can do to make up for it?

12. The doctor _____ a light in the unconscious woman's eyes to try to get her to react.

13. I think it's disgusting when reporters write _____ stories about violent crimes.

Word Families

A **root** of a word is a part of a word with a specific meaning. For example, the target word **sensational** contains the root *sen*, which comes from the Latin word meaning "sense" or "feel." Like other roots, *sen* appears as a part of many words, but it is not used alone.

Read these sentences. The boldfaced words all contain the root *sen*. Can you guess what the words mean? Write a definition for each one. Compare your definitions with a classmate's. Then, check your definitions in a dictionary.

1. I don't like **sentimental** birthday cards. I prefer humorous cards.

   _____

2. After the accident, he lost all **sensation** in his left hand.

   _____

3. When anyone comes close to the house, the outside lights come on immediately because they are connected to a motion **sensor**.

   _____

> ### Studying Collocations
>
> There are many collocations associated with driving. In this chapter, you learned the collocation **pull in front of**.

Read the following sentences and look at the pictures. Can you guess the meaning of the boldfaced phrases? Write one phrase next to each picture.

1. She **pulled off** the road to make a call.
2. The movie is at 7:00, so I'll **pick you up** at 6:30.
3. The other driver gestured angrily when we **cut him off**.
4. At the next corner, **take a left**. My house is the first one on the right.
5. This is a **one-way street**!

1. _____

2. _____

3. _____

4. _____

5. _____

PUTTING IT ALL TOGETHER

Discussion

Share your ideas in a small group.

1. Design a television advertisement to introduce "the Flash" to the public. Use at least five of the target words from the chapter. Perform your advertisement for the class.

2. Complete the scale showing how aggressive you think drivers are in different regions of the world. Use the abbreviations listed below. You do not have to use all of the positions on the scale, and you can place more than one region in the same position. When you finish, compare your group's scale to those of other groups. Be ready to explain your answers. As you talk, try to use the vocabulary below. Each time someone uses a target word or phrase, put a check (✓) next to it.

accuse	damage	gesture	incident	injured	insurance
legal	pull in front of	rage	range	vehicle	witness

How aggressive do you think drivers are in different regions of the world?

Eastern Europe (EE)	Western Europe (WE)	Far East (FE)
Southeast Asia (SEA)	Middle East (ME)	North America (NA)
Central and South America (CSA)		

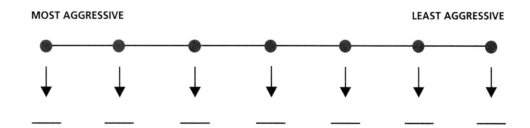

Writing

Complete one or both of these writing topics. When you write, use at least five of the target words from the chapter. Underline the target words in your paper.

1. Imagine that you live in a city where there have recently been several serious incidents of road rage. Write a letter to the city official who is in charge of traffic. Make suggestions about what the city or town can do to reduce the number of road rage incidents.

2. What do you think about the punishment that Tracy Alfieri received? Was it severe enough? Was it too severe? Write an essay expressing your opinion. Include specific reasons to support your ideas. If you use information from the reading in your essay, paraphrase it—do not copy it.

Wrap-up

REVIEWING READING SKILLS AND VOCABULARY

Read the text. Do not use a dictionary.

1   People with expressive faces are probably not surprised when others sometimes "read their minds." However, even those who are not at all reserved can usually control their facial expressions if they make a conscious attempt. But imagine what your life would be like if anyone observing you could know exactly what you were thinking and feeling. What if your every emotion—guilt, shame, shock, anger, disgust, fear— immediately flashed across your face, for the whole world to witness. For people who suffer from a condition known as chronic blushing, this unfortunate situation is an everyday reality.

2   Of course, it is normal for our faces to become hot and get red when we are embarrassed. However, for people who suffer from chronic blushing, this normal physical reaction to stress is so constant and severe that it can damage their personal and professional lives. Consider, for example, a young television news announcer just starting out in her career. She has always blushed easily, but suddenly, she notices that whenever she reports on a tragic, sensational, or even humorous incident, her face, neck, and ears all turn a deep red. At first she deals with the problem by putting heavy makeup on her face before going on television. Unfortunately, the makeup gives her an artificial appearance, and she begins to lose popularity with television viewers.

3   The story of the television news announcer is just one of many that reveals the negative effect that chronic blushing can have on one's life. So, what can someone who suffers from this condition do? For minor cases, makeup works quite well. For serious cases, there is an operation that can get rid of blushing. However, it is a major operation that most doctors will perform only after the patient has explored other solutions.

Comprehension Check

Read these sentences. Circle T (true) , F (false), or ? (can't determine the answer from the reading). If you circle F, change the sentence to make it true.

1. Most people are able to hide their feelings if they try hard enough.   T   F   ?

2. Blushing is very common.   T   F   ?

3. People who blush too much can sometimes have personal and professional problems.   T   F   ?

163

4. Chronic blushers are much more emotional than other people.   T   F   ?

5. According to the writer, people who suffer from chronic blushing should have an operation to correct the problem.   T   F   ?

Guessing Meaning from Context

Answer these questions.

1. What is **chronic blushing**? (paragraph 1)

_____

2. What is **makeup**? (paragraph 2)

_____

3. What does **minor** mean? (paragraph 3)

_____

4. What target word from the unit is the adjective **tragic** related to? What does **tragic** mean? (paragraph 2)

_____

Understanding Inference

Use inference to answer these questions.

1. What are three jobs in which chronic blushing might be a serious problem? For each job, explain how chronic blushing might be a serious disadvantage.

_____

_____

2. Imagine a case in which a doctor refused to perform an operation to "cure" someone's blushing problem. Describe the case using specific details.

_____

_____

Paraphrasing

Paraphrase these sentences from the text.

1. People with expressive faces are probably not surprised when others sometimes "read their minds."

_____

2. Of course, it is normal for our faces to become hot and get red when we are embarrassed.

_____

3. However, it is a major operation that most doctors will perform only after the patient has explored other solutions.

_____

EXPANDING VOCABULARY

Studying Collocations

Read these sentences, and look carefully at the pattern for each verb.

a. Our company can **insure** you **against** fire but not against damage due to wind.

   Pattern = **insure** someone or something **against** something

b. He **accused** me **of** being dishonest.

   Pattern = **accuse** someone **of** something (or of doing something)

c. I always **associate** the smell of rain **with** my farm.

   Pattern = **associate** something or someone **with** something or someone else

d. Could you please **translate** this **from** English **into** Chinese?

   Pattern = **translate** something **from** something (a language) **into** something else (another language)

e. The cost of a house in this town **ranges from** $175,000 **to** $400,000.

   Pattern = something **ranges from** something (an amount or size) **to** something else (another amount or size)

On a separate piece of paper, answer these questions in complete sentences. Use the boldfaced verb and preposition combinations.

1. If you live on the beach, what should you be **insured against**?
2. If the police **accused** you **of** something you didn't do, what would you do?
3. What smell(s) do you **associate with** your childhood?
4. Is it easy or difficult for you to **translate something from** your first language **into** English?
5. In your city, what does it cost to rent a one-bedroom apartment? (Use **range from** . . . **to** in your answer.)

Word Families

Some words can be nouns or verbs, with no change in spelling.

Complete the sentences with the words in the box. Identify whether the word is used as a noun or a verb. Circle N (noun) or V (verb).

| damage | gesture | honor | range |

1. Why did you _____ at me?   N   V

   I'm not familiar with the _____ that you used.   N   V

2. How did you _____ my computer?   N   V

   The _____ will be expensive to repair.   N   V

3. They had a party to _____ their employees.   N   V

   The employees were proud of the _____.   N   V

4. The salary _____ in their department is quite wide.   N   V

   The salaries _____ from $35,000 to $100,000.   N   V

PLAYING WITH WORDS

Look back at the lists of target vocabulary on pages 132, 143, and 155. In a small group, write as many target words and phrases as you can under each category shown in the chart below. Be ready to explain your answers. Some words might fit under more than one category, and some words might not fit under any category.

Things you can touch and see	Ways of showing your emotions
vehicle	
Bad feelings, behavior, or qualities	**Good feelings, behavior, or qualities**
	honor

BUILDING DICTIONARY SKILLS

Finding Words in the Dictionary

When you look up a word, you can find information about other words in the same word family in the same entry or in nearby entries. For example, look at the dictionary entries on page 167.

> **con·scious** /'kanʃəs/ *adj* **1** noticing or realizing something; AWARE: *Jodie was very conscious of the fact that he was watching her.* **2** awake and able to understand what is happening around you: *Owen was still conscious when they arrived at the hospital.* **3** intended or planned: *Jenny made a **conscious effort/decision** to smoke less.* **-consciously** *adv* -opposite UNCONSCIOUS¹
>
> **con·scious·ness** /'kanʃəsnɪs/ *n* [U] **1** the condition of being awake and understanding what is happening around you: *Charlie fell down the stairs and **lost consciousness**.* **2** the understanding that you or a group of people have about a situation: *a **consciousness raising** effort* (=effort to make people understand and care about a problem)

Above the entry for the target word **consciousness,** you find the entry for the related adjective **conscious.** You also find the adverb form **consciously,** and an adjective with the opposite meaning, **unconscious.**

Look up the words in the box in your dictionary and find other forms of each word. Fill in the blanks with the correct forms of the words.

accuse	associate	calculate	injure	legal
muscle	observe	recognize	tragedy	translate

1. Your <u>calculations</u>_____ are correct, but your final answer is incorrect. Check your numbers again.

2. Your _____ is not very serious, but you won't be able to use your hand for a few days.

3. He has strong, _____ legs because he rides his bicycle every day to work.

4. The doctor made a _____ mistake, and as a result his patient died.

5. Can you help me with this _____? My Spanish isn't very good.

6. After watching the animals for several hours, the researcher wrote down her _____ in a notebook. Later her assistant typed them for her.

7. He said he knew her, but I think he was lying. When he saw her, there was no _____ on his face.

8. You can't do that! It's _____!

9. The police will never believe your _____. You have no proof!

10. If you belong to the Automobile _____ and you have a problem with your car while you are on a trip, you can call them for help.

UNIT 5

MAN AND BEAST

CHAPTER 13

Is Music Universal?

Many whales communicate with each other with "whale songs."

GETTING READY TO READ

A Do you think the following statements are true or false? Write T (true) or F (false). Compare your answers with a partner.

_____ **1.** Everyone defines music the same way.

_____ **2.** It is possible that historically, humans learned how to play music before they learned how to speak.

_____ **3.** A wide variety of animal species both make music and seem to enjoy it.

_____ **4.** Whale "songs" are completely different from human songs.

_____ **5.** Some animals make their own musical instruments and play them.

_____ **6.** There is one part of the brain that is used specifically for music.

B The **boldfaced** words and phrases in the paragraph below appear in the reading. Which words are new to you? Circle them. Then, work with a partner. Read this paragraph introducing the topic of the reading, and match the words with their definitions.

There is a lot of evidence that humans' love for music is quite **ancient**, perhaps even as old as the human race. However, there is now evidence that not only humans but also many other **species** of animals have a basic **appreciation** for music. In the **journal** *Science*, several **biologists** have written about how the brains of humans and animals react to music in very similar ways. The researchers hope that their work on the way that music affects the brain will lead to developments that could one day help **the deaf** to hear.

Word	Definition
_____ **1.** biologists	**a.** a group of animals or plants of the same kind that can breed (have babies) with each other
_____ **2.** journal	**b.** belonging to a long time ago; very old
_____ **3.** species	**c.** scientists who study living things
_____ **4.** appreciation	**d.** people who can't hear
_____ **5.** the deaf	**e.** a magazine or newspaper for people who are interested in a particular subject
_____ **6.** ancient	**f.** an understanding of the importance or meaning of something

READING

Read the text once without stopping.

Is Music Universal?

1   It has long been said that music is universal, but now science is proving just how deeply true that statement really is. Like most people, scientists cannot define exactly what music is, but they know it when they hear it. One group of scientists has shown that human **appreciation** of music may be shared by whales, birds, and even rats; that it is remarkably **ancient;** and that studying why animals and humans appreciate music may help us better understand how the brain works.

2   In research published in 2001 in the **journal** *Science,* several scientists have shown that in very basic ways other **species** share music

continued

appreciation and that this appreciation may be one of humanity's oldest activities. Through such research, scientists hope they may come to understand the human mind better, perhaps even learning **key** information about how to deal with damage to the **auditory system**.

3   Jelle Atema is a **biologist** and coauthor of one of the *Science* papers.[1] Like several of the researchers involved in the *Science* papers, Atema is both a scientist and a musician. In addition to his work in biology, he plays the flute.[2] He has carefully made exact copies of ancient bone flutes in order to play them. He wants to determine the kinds of sounds that early humans may have made. Another of the researchers, Harvard Medical School's Mark Jude Tramo, is also a talented guitarist.

4   "Do musical sounds in nature reveal a profound[3] **bond** between all living things?" asks one of the papers. There is a lot of **evidence** that perhaps it does. For example, the "songs" of one type of whale follow many of the same, **precise** rules that are nearly universal in human music. The general **structure** of whale music is remarkably similar to that of human music. For example, the two species share a similar tonal[4] **scale**, and their songs involve the introduction and variation of a central **theme**.

5   Many species of birds sing in ways that also follow the rules of human song, including the ways that songs are passed from one generation to another or are shared by a group of peers. Many use note scales similar to those used by humans, even though an **endless** variety of such scales is possible. Some even make instruments and play them. For example, one type of bird uses a **hollow** log[5] as a **drum**, beating on it with a small stick it breaks off from a tree!

6   Music goes back to the earliest ages of human prehistory,[6] and flutes have been found that may be 53,000 years old. The technology used to make these ancient instruments was much more advanced, Atema says, than that used at the same period to produce tools. "To see that they spent so much time [making instruments] means music was important to them," he says. The ability to make music, some scientists believe, may even be older than language.

continued

---

[1] a *paper* = a piece of writing by researchers who have made a study of a particular subject

[2] a *flute* = a musical instrument shaped like a pipe, that you play by holding it across your lips and blowing into it

[3] *profound* = having a strong influence or effect

[4] *tonal* = having a particular quality of musical sound

[5] a *log* = a thick piece of wood cut from a tree

[6] *prehistory* = the time in history before anything was written down

7   Tramo, a neurologist[7] at Harvard Medical School and Massachusetts General Hospital, says he is fascinated by the complexity of the human brain's reaction to music. "There is no 'music center' in the brain," he wrote. Nearly every thinking part of the brain is involved in listening to music, and when we move to the music many of the areas controlling movement are involved too. "Imagine how much of the brain lights up when we dance!"

8   Tramo sees the research on music as a process leading to a better understanding of how the brain works. By learning exactly how the brain processes and "understands" the specific features that music is made of, a more complete understanding of how the brain **makes sense of** the world around us may develop. In the same way, other scientists are using the way the brain reacts to **visual** arts as a way of understanding the way the human visual system works.

9   Tramo believes that, "That understanding . . . is going to help scientists in their efforts to help **the deaf** to hear, and help the blind to see."

_____

[7] a _neurologist_ = a doctor who studies and treats the nervous system and the diseases related to it

Comprehension Check

Read these sentences. Circle T (true) or F (false). If you circle F, change the sentence to make it true. When you finish, go back and compare your answers to the way you answered on page 169. Then, check your answers with a classmate. If your answers are different, look back at the reading.

1. Everyone defines music the same way.   T   F

2. It is possible that historically, humans learned how to   T   F
    play music before they learned how to speak.

3. A wide variety of animal species both make music   T   F
    and seem to enjoy it.

4. Whale "songs" are completely different from human   T   F
    songs.

5. Some animals make their own musical instruments   T   F
    and play them.

6. There is one part of the brain that is used specifically   T   F
    for music.

EXPLORING VOCABULARY

Thinking about the Vocabulary

Guessing Strategy

Sometimes, a word is followed by a descriptive phrase that can help you guess its meaning. Look at the example.

> The scientist submitted an article to the **journal**, writing about music's effects on babies' development.

From the descriptive phrase after the word *journal*, you should be able to figure out that a journal is something that contains written articles.

Try It!

Read the sentence, and write a definition of the **boldfaced** target word.

> Some even make instruments and play them. For example, one type of bird uses a hollow log as a **drum**, beating on it with a small stick it breaks off from a tree!

Drum means _____

Look at the target words and phrases. Which ones are new to you? Circle them here and in the reading. Then read "Is Music Universal?" again. Look at the context of each new word and phrase. Can you guess the meaning? Use the Guessing Strategy where possible.

Target Words and Phrases

appreciation (1)	**auditory** (2)	**precise** (4)	**hollow** (5)
ancient (1)	**system** (2)	**structure** (4)	**drum** (5)
journal (2)	**biologist** (2)	**scale** (4)	**makes sense of** (8)
species (2)	**bond** (4)	**theme** (4)	**visual** (8)
key (2)	**evidence** (4)	**endless** (5)	**the deaf** (9)

Using the Vocabulary

These sentences are about the reading. What is the meaning of each boldfaced word or phrase? Circle a, b, or c. Circle the words or phrases in the sentences that help you understand the meanings of the target words.

1. Scientists have recently found **evidence** that some animals produce music very similar to human music. One example is the fact that whale songs follow many of the same musical patterns as human songs. *Evidence* is used to

    a. conduct an experiment.

    b. prove a theory.

    c. make music.

2. There is an **endless** variety of musical patterns. It is therefore surprising that human songs and whale songs are so similar. If something is *endless*, it

    a. hurts your ears because it is so loud.

    b. is very large or very long.

    c. is so difficult that no one can understand it.

3. An example of a similarity between whale music and human music is the **scale** that they both use. Although the number of possible musical **scales** is in fact endless, both whales and humans "sing" with the same notes. A musical *scale* is

    a. a combination of a variety of animal sounds.

    b. a musical note that is sung for a long time.

    c. a series of notes that go from lower to higher or from higher to lower in a set pattern.

4. Like humans, whales begin their songs with a **theme**, make some changes to it, and then come back to the original **theme** before ending the song. The *theme* of a piece of music is

    a. the main subject of it.

    b. the first note of it.

    c. the most popular song in it.

5. In fact, both whale and human music follow many of the same, very **precise** rules. If a rule is *precise*, it is

    a. exact and correct in every detail.

    b. important in a very general way.

    c. interesting and beautiful.

6. Another fascinating similarity between human and animal music is that some animals actually make musical instruments. For example, one bird uses a stick to hit an empty piece of wood, or **drum**, with it. A *drum* is a musical instrument that

    a. sounds like a bird's song.

    b. is played by hitting it with the hand or an object.

    c. makes a very soft, continuous sound.

7. Interestingly, the bird only uses the stick to hit a **hollow** piece of wood. It never chooses a solid piece of wood. A *hollow* piece of wood is

   a. very heavy.   **b.** extremely dry.   **c.** empty inside.

8. All of this evidence of musical similarities between animals and humans suggests that the **bond** between us and other living things is deeper than we thought. A *bond* is a

   a. connection.   **b.** difference.   **c.** suggestion.

9. By studying how the brains of both humans and animals process music, scientists hope to learn **key** information about the way the brain works in general. *Key* information is

   a. very difficult.   **b.** very important.   **c.** very new.

10. Scientists hope to use this information to help people who are deaf. They hope to learn how to repair damage to parts of the **auditory system** such as the inner ear. The *auditory system* includes

    a. the parts of the body that have been injured.   **b.** the parts of the body that enable us to hear.   **c.** the internal (inside) parts of the body.

11. While some scientists are working to help the deaf, others are working to help the blind. They are trying to better understand the way the human **visual** system works. Our *visual* system is in charge of

    a. what and how we see.   **b.** what and how we hear.   **c.** what and how we move.

12. Scientists want to know how the brain **makes sense of** the visual and auditory information it receives. When you *make sense of* something, you

    a. understand how it works.   **b.** improve the way it works.   **c.** hear it and watch it.

13. Despite progress in science and technology, scientists still do not completely understand the **structure** of the human brain. If they could understand the brain's *structure*, they would understand

    a. the way it is organized.   **b.** what happens when we die.   **c.** how to control it.

DEVELOPING READING SKILLS

Understanding Main Ideas, Major Points, and Supporting Details

An **outline** gives you an overall idea of the structure and most important information in a text. You can look at an outline of a reading and immediately recognize the relationship among the main ideas, major points, and supporting details. When you write an outline, you should use single words or phrases rather than full sentences.

This is an outline of the information contained in paragraphs 4 and 5 of "Is Music Universal?". Fill in the missing information in the outline. The Roman numeral I is for the main idea, the letters A and B are for the major points, and the numbers 1, 2, 3, and 4 are for the supporting details.

    I. _____

        A. <u>Structure of whale music and human music is very similar.</u>

            1. _____

            2. _____

        B. _____

            1. _____

            2. <u>Share songs with peers.</u>

            3. _____

            4. _____

Summarizing

Use the information from your outline to write a summary of paragraphs 4 and 5 of the reading. Do not look back at the text.

EXPANDING VOCABULARY

Using the Vocabulary in New Contexts

These sentences use the target words and phrases **in new contexts**.
Complete them with the words and phrases in the box.

auditory	bond	drums	endless	evidence	hollow	key
make sense of	precise	scale	structure	system	themes	visual

1. He was in a car accident and suffered severe _____ damage.
   Now he's deaf.

2. The _____ between mother and child is very strong. Even
   when they live far away from each other, they always feel a connection.

3. He went to a special institute for _____ arts. He studied
   painting and design.

4. What is the highest note that you can sing on a C major _____?

5. That movie seemed _____! I was really bored.

6. This lamp looks heavy, but actually it's very light because it's

   _____.

7. If you are having trouble dancing to the music, just listen for the

   _____.

8. I can't _____ these instructions. Can you help me?

9. The police can't prove he robbed the bank because they don't have any

   _____.

10. Maintaining group harmony is a _____ feature of Japanese
    culture.

11. Courts, lawyers, and judges are key parts of the legal _____.

12. Because of client complaints, the management is changing the company
    _____. They will have fewer supervisors and more customer
    service help.

13. I don't like movies that deal with serious _____. I prefer
    movies that make me laugh.

14. Please check your calculations. The measurement must be

    _____.

> **Word Families**
>
> In Chapter 12, you learned that a root is a part of a word with a specific meaning. The target word **biologist** contains the root *bio,* which means "life." The target words **visual** and **auditory** contain roots too: *vis* means "see"; *audi* means "hear."

Ⓐ **Read these sentences. Match the boldfaced words with their definitions.**

1. My night **vision** is not very good. I need to wear glasses when I drive after dark.
2. The **audience** loved his performance. Everyone in the theater stood up and clapped when he finished.
3. Do you need any **audiovisual** equipment for your presentation?
4. In the past ten years, scientists have made a lot of progress in the field of **biotechnology**.
5. Do you think the professor will let me **audit** her course? I don't need a grade; I just want to attend her lectures.

Word	Definition
_____ **1.** vision	**a.** the people watching or listening to a concert, speech, movie, etc.
_____ **2.** audience	**b.** the ability to see
_____ **3.** audiovisual	**c.** study a subject at college without getting a grade for it
_____ **4.** biotechnology	**d.** the use of living things such as cells in science and industry
_____ **5.** audit	**e.** involving the use of recorded pictures and sound

Ⓑ **Working with a partner, answer the questions using the boldfaced words.**

1. Is your night **vision** as good as your day **vision**?
2. Have you ever performed in front of a live **audience**? If not, would you like to? Why or why not?
3. In which professions are **audiovisual** presentations common?
4. What kinds of research are being done in the field of **biotechnology**?
5. In universities in your country, is it possible to **audit** classes? What are the advantages and disadvantages of auditing a class?

Studying Collocations

There are many collocations with the word **system**. A **system** is a set of related or connected things that work together. The human body, for example, has systems that consist of organs that work together. The **auditory** and **visual** systems are two of the body's systems. Other systems of the body include the circulatory system and the digestive system. There are also government systems. The educational system and the legal system are two important government systems.

Work with a partner. Write each word under the category that you associate the word with. Some words may go in more than one category. For example, you may associate the word _knowledge_ with just the educational system. Somebody else might put it in all four categories, because knowledge is important to all of the systems. Be ready to explain your associations.

athlete	blood	diet	disease
evidence	freedom	heart	instructor
judge	justice	knowledge	laboratory
lawyer	literature	misidentify	peer
physical	poison	prescribe	prevent
proof	research	stomach	victim
witness			

Educational system	Circulatory system	Digestive system	Legal system
knowledge	heart	stomach	

PUTTING IT ALL TOGETHER

Discussion

Share your ideas in a small group. As you talk, try to use the vocabulary below. Each time someone uses a target word or phrase, put a check (✓) next to it.

appreciation/appreciate	auditory	audience	bond	drum
make sense of	scale	species	structure	system
theme				

1. How is music important to individuals? To society? Make a list of all the ways people use music. For example, you could write: *People use music to relax.* Try to think of at least six things.

2. Now make a list of all the ways animals use music. Can you think of anything that animals might use music for that humans do not?

Writing

Complete one or both of these writing topics. When you write, use at least five of the target words from the chapter. Underline the target words in your paper.

1. Do some research at the library or on the Internet on whale songs or bird songs. Then, write a short report on what you have learned. Do not copy from the research—paraphrase.

2. Imagine that you have traveled to a planet where music does not exist. Write a letter to a friend on earth explaining what life is like without music.

CHAPTER 14

Our Dogs Are Watching Us

Can dogs read our minds?

GETTING READY TO READ

A **Talk with a partner or in a small group.**

1. Do you now, or have you ever had a pet? If so, tell your group about your pet. If not, would you like to have a pet? Why or why not?

2. Do you think that it is possible for animals and people to have an emotional connection? Explain your answer.

3. Which animals are best at communicating with people? Complete the chart.

   dogs   **horses**   **cats**   **birds**

   Other (your ideas): _____

Very good at communicating with people	Can communicate with people, but not very well	Can't communicate with people

B The **boldfaced** words and phrases in the paragraph below appear in the reading. Which words are new to you? Circle them. Then, work with a partner. Read this paragraph introducing the topic of the reading, and match the words with their definitions.

Can dogs **read the minds** of their human owners? To anyone who owns a dog, the answer is **obvious**: Yes! Now, scientists have done some interesting experiments to **back up** the theory that as dogs **evolved** from their wolf ancestors over thousands of years, they developed a simple, yet **striking** characteristic. They learned to look at people's faces, something that wolves rarely or never do.

Word	Definition
_____ **1.** read (someone's) mind	**a.** unusual or interesting enough to be noticed
_____ **2.** obvious	**b.** develop by changing slowly over time
_____ **3.** back up	**c.** show that something is true
_____ **4.** evolve	**d.** guess what someone is thinking
_____ **5.** striking	**e.** easy to notice or understand

READING

Read the text once without stopping.

Our Dogs Are Watching Us

ADAPTED FROM: Ingram, Jay. "Dogs keep eyes on the prize by watching us." *Toronto Star* 18 May 2003: E06.

1   A few months ago, I reported a study of the abilities of dogs to **read the minds** of their owners. Well, not exactly. They were not really reading minds; they were reading human body language to figure out which of two containers actually had food hidden in it. Now, experimenters have conducted more research in an attempt to identify the single skill that dogs have but other animals lack.

2   In experiments reported in November 2002, scientists compared dogs, wolves,[1] and **chimpanzees**. The tests involved hiding food in one of two

continued

---

[1] a *wolf* = a wild animal that looks like a dog and lives and hunts in groups

containers, then pointing at, looking at, or both pointing at and tapping[2] on the container with the food.

3   While dogs were quick to figure out which container held what they were looking for, neither the wolves nor the chimps understood what the experimenters were trying to communicate. The inability of the chimps to perform better than the dogs was surprising, considering the **overall** intelligence of chimpanzees. But the differences between dogs and wolves were fascinating because of the relationship between the two.

4   Wolves gave rise to[3] dogs several thousand years ago, and while the physical differences between the two are the most **obvious**, there are clearly mental differences, too. This experiment suggested those differences are in the area of social interaction with humans. A team of Hungarian scientists has found what they think is the key: Dogs look at people's faces. It sounds simple, but there are experiments to **back up** the claim.

5   The Hungarian team made sure that the wolves were **socialized** to humans by having them live with people 24 hours a day from the time they were four days old. This meant that the dogs and wolves **were** equally **used to** human voices and gestures. By **familiarizing** the wolves and dogs to humans, the researchers hoped to **eliminate** the effect that the animals' anxiety might have on the experiment. The socialization seems to have worked. Some of the wolves were able to understand some of the human gestures, although overall they still were not as good as the dogs.

6   It was a second experiment that revealed the key difference between the two animals. Both dogs and wolves were trained to get a piece of meat in two ways. They were taught how to lift the **lid** of a container to get at the meat inside and how to pull a rope (tied around a piece of meat) out of a cage.[4] When the animals had figured out how to do both, the scientists tricked them: The lid was **fastened** down and the rope was tied to the cage. It was now impossible for them to get at the food.

7   What happened? I'm sorry I can't report that the dogs learned to untie the rope or use a screwdriver[5] to open the container, but they did do something the wolves didn't do—they kept looking at the people in the room, apparently[6] waiting for some sort of sign to help them get the meat.

continued

---

[2] *tap* = gently hit your finger against something

[3] *gave rise to* = were the species that (dogs) evolved from

[4] a *cage* = a structure made of wires or bars in which birds or animals can be kept

[5] a *screwdriver* = a tool with a long, thin metal end, used for turning screws (a piece of metal used to keep two pieces of wood or metal together)

[6] *apparently* = according to the way something looks or someone appears

8   The differences between the two animals were **striking**. In both tests, seven out of nine dogs kept **checking out** the person, while only two out of seven wolves did. The researchers claim that this act of looking at human faces is a "genetic predisposition" in dogs. It is one of the **innate** differences between the two species and therefore must have been one of the first steps in the process of **domestication** thousands of years ago.

9   I would like to see this new piece of evidence applied to previous observations and theories about how dogs were domesticated. Some researchers have theorized that as dogs evolved from wolves, their behavior became more **immature**. For instance, dogs exhibit[7] submissive[8] behaviors that wolves do not, as if adult dogs are more like baby wolves. But the tests conducted by the Hungarian researchers were done when the animals were only a few months old, so you would think that if dog behavior is basically the same as that of young wolves, the wolves in this experiment might have looked at their owners, too.

10   I can add to this research from my own experience. My dog also looks at people to get food: He makes sure I'm not looking at him, then steals my sandwich. That's what I call highly **evolved** behavior.

----

[7] *exhibit* = show or display

[8] *submissive* = always willing to obey someone

Comprehension Check

Read these sentences. Circle T (true), F (false), or ? (can't determine the answer from the reading). If you circle F, change the sentence to make it true. Check your answers with a classmate. If your answers are different, look back at the reading.

1. The experiments proved that dogs are more intelligent than chimpanzees.   T   F   ?

2. The experiments showed that there are very specific differences between dogs and wolves.   T   F   ?

3. The experiments showed that wolves and dogs are not related.   T   F   ?

4. In the second experiment, the dogs who looked at the experimenters were given a piece of meat as a reward.   T   F   ?

5. The behavior of young wolves and young dogs is basically the same.   T   F   ?

6. Some researchers believe that dogs have a special ability to understand human beings.   T   F   ?

EXPLORING VOCABULARY

Thinking about the Vocabulary

Guessing Strategy

You learned in the **Guessing Strategy** for Chapter 10 that words can have similar meanings even if they are not the same word form. Look at the example.

> The Hungarian team **socialized** the wolves to humans by having them live with people 24 hours a day from the time they were four days old. By **familiarizing** the wolves and dogs to humans, the researchers hoped to eliminate the effect that the animals' anxiety might have on the experiment.

Based on the context, you can guess that the words *socialized* and *familiarizing* have a similar meaning, even though one is a verb in the past tense, while the other is a gerund.

Try It!

Read the sentence, and write the word that is similar in meaning to the **boldfaced** target word.

> There are several **striking** differences between dog and wolf behavior. For example, researchers noticed that dogs look at human faces, while wolves don't.

Striking is similar in meaning to _____

Look at the target words and phrases. Which ones are new to you? Circle them here and in the reading. Then read "Our Dogs Are Watching Us" again. Look at the context of each new word and phrase. Can you guess the meaning? Use the Guessing Strategy where possible.

Target Words and Phrases

read the minds (1)	socialized (5)	lid (6)	innate (8)
chimpanzees (2)	were used to (5)	fastened (6)	domestication (8)
overall (3)	familiarizing (5)	striking (8)	immature (9)
obvious (4)	eliminate (5)	checking out (8)	evolved (10)
back up (4)			

Using the Vocabulary

These sentences are **about the reading**. Complete them with the words and phrases in the box. Circle the words or phrases in the sentences that help you understand the meanings of the target words.

checked out	chimpanzees	domestication	eliminate	familiarize	fastening
immature	innate	lid	overall	socialized	used to

1. Some recent experiments involving dogs, _____, and wolves show that dogs might have a special ability to communicate with humans.

2. Although chimps are considered to be more intelligent than dogs _____, dogs are better in at least one way—communicating with humans.

3. The _____ of the wolf over thousands of years led to the development of a new species, the dog.

4. Dogs might have an _____ trait that helps them communicate with humans. It is likely that they were born with this characteristic because even very young, or _____, dogs seem to have this trait.

5. Dogs often interact with humans, but wolves do not. Therefore, when comparing wolf and dog behavior, researchers had to first _____ the wolves to people. They had to make sure that the young wolves felt as comfortable with people as the young dogs did.

6. The experimenters made sure that the wolves were _____ to humans by having them live with people 24 hours a day from the time they were four days old.

7. The scientists wanted to make sure that both the wolves and the dogs felt comfortable with people. They wanted to _____ any difference between the wolves' relationships to people and the dogs' relationships to people.

8. By the time the scientists did the experiment, the wolves were comfortable with human beings. They were _____ human voices and gestures.

9. In one experiment, the scientists trained the animals to open the _____ of a container to get at the food inside.

10. Then, by _____ the top of the container, the experimenters made it impossible for the animals to open it.

11. When they couldn't open the container, most of the dogs _____ the experimenters' faces, but only two of the wolves looked at the people.

DEVELOPING READING SKILLS

Understanding Details

Look at the illustrations. Write a 1 below those that correspond to the first experiment, a 2 below those that correspond to the second set of experiments, a 1 and a 2 below those that correspond to both experiments, and an X below those that do not correspond to either experiment.

a. _____

b. _____

c. _____

d. _____

e. _____

f. _____

Recognizing Tone

One important element of any text is the writer's **tone** or attitude. To identify a writer's tone, you can ask yourself a series of questions. For example: Is the writer serious? playful? worried? funny? critical? angry? sad? Why does the writer use this tone? What is his or her purpose?

Look at the last paragraph of the reading. What is the tone of the paragraph? Why does the writer use this tone? Where else in the reading does the writer use a similar tone? Write the paragraph number.

_____

_____

EXPANDING VOCABULARY

Using the Vocabulary in New Contexts

These sentences use the target words and phrases **in new contexts**.
Complete them with the words and phrases in the box.

check out	chimpanzees	domestication	eliminate	familiarize	fasten
immature	innate	lid	overall	socialization	used to

1. Please _____ your seatbelt. The plane is about to land.

2. Humans and _____ are very similar genetically. In fact, they are our closest animal relative.

3. Some researchers believe that an appreciation for music is an _____ human trait.

4. Please make sure the _____ of the trash can is tightly closed.

5. The _____ of horses made it possible for humans to travel over longer distances.

6. The _____ of young children is an important goal of any educational system. In school, children are taught to interact with their peers.

7. This cake is too sweet. The next time I make it, I'm going to _____ some of the sugar from the recipe.

8. When I got my new computer, it took me about a week to _____ myself with all of its different features.

9. Your _____ behavior is not acceptable. You are not a little boy anymore.

10. Scientists don't understand precisely how the brain makes sense of music, but they do have a good understanding of the _____ structure of the auditory system.

11. Hey, _____ this website. It's really interesting.

12. When I first moved from New York to London, it was difficult for me to drive on the left side of the road, but now I'm _____ it.

Word Families

In Chapters 10 and 12 you learned about paraphrasing. When you paraphrase, one of the ways to change the structure of the original sentence without changing its meaning is to use a different form of one of the words in the original sentence. Look at the example.

> *Original sentence*: It took thousands of years for dogs to **evolve** from wolves.
> *Paraphrase*: The **evolution** of the dog from its wolf ancestor took many, many years.

Study the chart. Then look at the sentences below. In each set of sentences, b is a paraphrase of a. Complete the paraphrases with the appropriate forms of the words from the chart. Make sure that your paraphrases are grammatically correct and have the same meaning. Be careful; you will not use all the words.

Noun	Verb	Adjective
domestication	domesticate	domestic
evolution	evolve	
familiarity	familiarize	familiar
immaturity		immature
socialization	socialize	social

1. **a.** Scientists used to believe that dogs were just a _____ form of the wolf.

    b. Until recently, scientists saw dogs as just wolves that ancient humans were able to _____.

2. **a.** The _____ that can be observed in adult dog behavior can be compared to the way that very young wolves act.

    b. The _____ behavior of mature dogs is similar to the behavior of wolves that are very young.

3. **a.** The dogs and the wolves had to have the same degree of _____ with humans before the experiment began.

    b. Both the dogs and the wolves had to be equally _____ with people before the researchers could start the experiment.

4. a. It is much easier to _____ a dog to humans than it is to do the same with a wolf.

  b. The _____ of wolves to people is far more difficult than getting a dog to adapt to people.

5. a. The _____ of a species is a process that involves many genetic changes.

  b. It takes a large number of changes in the genes of a species for it to _____.

Studying Word Grammar

The phrase **used to** can be used with both *be* and *get,* but the meaning is different. Look at the examples.

> I am the oldest of six children, so I **am used to** *sharing my things.* In contrast, my husband was an only child. He **is used to** *having his own things.* When we first got married, it wasn't easy to **get used to** *each other's habits.*

When you *are used to* something, you *are already* familiar with it. When you *get used to* something, you *become familiar with it over a period of time.* The same grammar patterns follow both *be* and *get used to.*

I **am used to sharing** everything. My husband had to **get used to sharing** his things with me.	*be* or *get* + *used to* + <u>gerund</u> (verb + *-ing*)
I had to **get used to my husband's habits.** It took a long time, but now we **are used to each other.**	*be* or *get* + *used to* + <u>direct object</u> (noun, pronoun, or noun phrase)

A Complete the sentences with *get* or *be.* Use the correct form of the verb.

1. I've tried, but I can't _____ used to eating with chopsticks.

2. Don't worry. It's difficult at first, but you will _____ used to driving on the left side.

3. At first, going to work so early was difficult for him, but now he _____ used to it.

4. I can't sleep at night if it's too quiet. I come from a big city, so I _____ used to falling asleep with a lot of traffic noise.

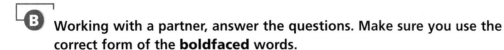

B Working with a partner, answer the questions. Make sure you use the correct form of the **boldfaced** words.

1. When two people get married, what are some of the things that they have to **get used to** about each other?

2. If you move to another country, what do you think will be the most difficult thing for you to **get used to**?

3. Tell your partner about something that was difficult for you to do at first, but that now you **are used to** doing.

PUTTING IT ALL TOGETHER

Discussion

Share your ideas in a small group. As you talk, try to use the vocabulary below. Each time someone uses a target word or phrase, put a check (✓) next to it.

chimpanzee/chimp	check out
domestic/domestication/domesticate	evolve/evolution
familiar/familiarity/familiarize	immature/immaturity/maturity/mature
innate	obvious
read someone's mind	socialize/socialization
striking	

1. Do you believe that animals and humans can communicate with each other? What kinds of things can they communicate? What kinds of things can't they communicate? Explain your answers with specific examples.

2. Your teacher will give your group blank copies of the questionnaire on the next page. Survey at least 10 pet owners (per group). Present your results to the class.

Gender of survey respondent:	☐ Male	☐ Female

1. What kind of pet do you have?

   ☐ dog   ☐ cat   ☐ bird   ☐ fish
   ☐ other (please specify): _____

2. How long have you had your pet?

   ☐ less than   ☐ 1–3 years   ☐ 4–6 years   ☐ more than
     a year   6 years

3. How many pets have you owned?

   ☐ just one   ☐ 2   ☐ 3 or more

4. How did you get your pet?

   ☐ I bought it.   ☐ It was a gift.   ☐ I found it.
   ☐ I got it from an animal shelter.*   ☐ Other? _____

5. How often do you talk to your pet?

   ☐ very often   ☐ sometimes   ☐ rarely   ☐ never

6. How well do you think your pet understands what you are thinking?

   ☐ very well   ☐ some   ☐ a little   ☐ not at all

7. How well do you think your pet understands what you are feeling?

   ☐ very well   ☐ some   ☐ a little   ☐ not at all

8. How much can your pet communicate to you about what it wants or needs?

   ☐ a lot   ☐ some things   ☐ not much   ☐ nothing

9. Do you think your pet loves you?

   ☐ yes   ☐ maybe   ☐ no

Writing

Complete one or both of these writing topics. When you write, use at least five of the target words from the chapter. Underline the target words in your paper.

1. Write a report based on your group's survey of pet owners. Try to explain the trends or patterns that you noticed in the data.

2. Do you think that the type of research reported on in the reading is important? Why or why not? Write an essay expressing your opinion about the value of this type of research.

_____

*an *animal shelter* = a building for animals without a place to live

CHAPTER 15

The Mind of the Chimpanzee

Jane Goodall with a baby chimp

GETTING READY TO READ

 A **Talk with a partner or in a small group.**

1. What skills do you think chimpanzees have? Put a check next to all that apply.

   _____ invent names for common objects   _____ recognize people after a long separation

   _____ understand human language   _____ use human language

   _____ paint pictures   _____ divide objects into categories

2. Chimpanzees are often used in laboratories in medical research projects. Some people believe that this is morally wrong and governments should not allow it. What do you think?

The **boldfaced** words and phrases in the paragraph below appear in the reading. Which words are new to you? Circle them. Then, work with a partner. Read this paragraph introducing the writer of the text, and match the words with their definitions.

Jane Goodall is a scientist who has spent her life living among and studying the behavior of our closest relative in the animal world—the chimpanzee. She has observed chimps for longer than any other scientist, and has spent endless hours **analyzing** the behavior of chimpanzees in **the wild**. She has also worked closely with other researchers who conduct experiments using domesticated chimps. In many of these experiments, the chimps are encouraged to **stretch** their minds to the limit, in order to see exactly how far their intellectual abilities can take them. Jane Goodall's work has led to discoveries that are **meaningful** not only to those involved in protecting wild animals, but also to anyone with an interest in human behavior.

	Word		Definition
_____	1. analyze	**a.**	an area that is natural and not controlled or changed by people
_____	2. the wild	**b.**	serious, useful, or important
_____	3. stretch	**c.**	examine or think about something carefully in order to understand it
_____	4. meaningful	**d.**	use as much of something as is available

READING

Read the text once without stopping.

The Mind of the Chimpanzee

ADAPTED FROM: Goodall, Jane. "The Mind of the Chimpanzee." *Through a Window.* Boston: Houghton Mifflin, 1990.

1   In the middle of the 1960s, Beatrice and Allen Gardner started a project that, along with other similar research, taught us a lot about the chimpanzee mind. They bought an **infant** chimpanzee and began to teach her the signs[1] of ASL, the American Sign Language used by many of the deaf in Canada and the United States. The Gardners achieved remarkable success with their student, Washoe. Not only did she learn signs easily, but she quickly began to put them together in **meaningful** ways. It was clear that when she saw or used a sign, she formed a picture in her mind of the object it represented. If, for example, she was

continued

_____

[1] a *sign* = a hand symbol used by the deaf to communicate

asked in sign language to get an apple, she would go and find an apple that was **out of sight** in another room.

2   When news of Washoe's achievements were first announced to the scientific community, there was a lot of **protest**. The results of the research **implied** that chimpanzees had the ability to learn a human language, and suggested that chimps might **possess** intellectual skills similar to those of humans. Although many were fascinated and excited by the Gardners' discoveries, many more **bitterly** criticized the whole project. The **controversy** led to many other language projects, and the resulting research provided additional information about the chimpanzee's mind.

3   The fact that chimpanzees have excellent memories surprised no one. So it was not particularly remarkable when Washoe gave the name-sign of Beatrice Gardner, her surrogate mother,[2] after a separation of 11 years. Actually, it was no greater an achievement than the memory of dogs who recognize their owners after separations of almost as long.

4   Chimpanzees also possess premathematical skills: they can, for example, easily tell the difference between *more* and *less.* They can put things into specific categories according to a particular characteristic. Therefore, they have no difficulty in separating a **pile** of food into fruits and vegetables at one time, and at another, dividing the same pile of food into *large* and *small,* even though this calls for putting some vegetables with some fruits.

5   Chimpanzees who have been taught a human language can **combine** signs creatively in order to describe objects for which they have no sign. Washoe, for example, **puzzled** the people taking care of her by asking many times for a *rock berry.* **Eventually** they discovered that she was referring to a sweet type of nut that she had been given for the first time a short time before. Another language-trained chimp described a cucumber[3] as a *green banana,* and another referred to an Alka-Seltzer[4] as a *listen drink.* They can even invent signs. One chimp had to be put on a leash[5] when she went outside. One day, ready to go outside but having no sign for *leash,* she showed what she wanted by holding a bent finger to the ring on her collar.[6] This sign became part of her vocabulary.

continued

---

[2] a *surrogate mother* = someone who takes the place of a person or animal's biological mother

[3] a *cucumber* = a long thin rounded vegetable with a dark green skin, usually eaten raw

[4] an *Alka-Seltzer* = a type of medicine that is put in water and then drunk, and that makes a sound when it is put in water

[5] a *leash* = a piece of rope, leather, etc. fastened to an animal's (usually a dog's) collar in order to control it

[6] a *collar* = a band put around an animal's neck

6   Some chimpanzees love to draw, and especially paint. Those who have learned sign language sometimes give a name to their artwork, "This apple"—or sweet corn, or bird, or whatever. The fact that the paintings often look, to our eyes, remarkably different from the objects themselves either means that the chimpanzees are not very good artists or that we have a lot to learn about chimpanzee art!

7   People sometimes ask why such complex intellectual powers have evolved in the chimpanzee when their lives in **the wild** are so simple. The answer is, of course, that their lives in the wild are not so simple! They use—and need—all their mental skills during normal everyday life in their complex society. Chimpanzees always have to make choices—where to go, or with whom to travel. They need highly developed social skills—particularly males who want to become leaders. And low-ranking[7] chimpanzees must learn to hide their intentions or to do things in secret if they want to survive. Indeed, the study of chimpanzees in the wild suggests that their intellectual abilities evolved over thousands of years to help them deal with daily life.

8   It is easier to study intellectual skill in the lab where, through carefully designed tests and the proper use of rewards, chimpanzees can be encouraged to **stretch** their minds to the limit. It is more meaningful to study the subject in the wild, but much harder. It is more meaningful because we can better understand the environmental pressures that led to the evolution of intellectual skills in chimpanzee societies. It is harder because, in the wild, almost all behaviors are complicated by endless variables;[8] years of observing, recording and **analyzing** replace planned testing; the number of research subjects can often be counted on the fingers of one hand; the only experiments are nature's own, and only time—eventually—may lead to their being repeated.

_____

[7] *low-ranking* = having a very low social position in a group

[8] a *variable* = something that may vary in different situations

Comprehension Check

Read these sentences. Circle T (true) or F (false). If you circle F, change the sentence to make it true. Check your answers with a classmate. If your answers are different, look back at the reading.

1. The Gardners got an infant chimpanzee as a pet.   T   F

2. Chimpanzees cannot learn how to use language.   T   F

3. The Gardners taught Washoe how to use ASL   T   F
    because she is deaf.

4. Dogs have better memories than chimpanzees. T F

5. Chimpanzees sometimes hide what they are thinking. T F

6. It is much easier to study a chimp in the laboratory than in the wild. T F

EXPLORING VOCABULARY

Thinking about the Vocabulary

Guessing Strategy

The use of similar structures in two sentences or phrases can provide important keys to understanding the meaning of unfamiliar vocabulary. Look at the example.

> The results of the research **implied** that chimpanzees had the ability to learn a human language, and suggested that chimps might **possess** intellectual skills similar to those of humans.

You can see a similarity between the phrase *implied that chimpanzees had the ability* and the phrase *suggested that chimps might possess intellectual skills . . .* By comparing the structure of the two phrases, you can infer that the target word *imply* is similar in meaning to *suggest,* and the target word *possess* is similar in meaning to *had.*

Try It!

Read the sentences, and write a definition of the **boldfaced** target word.

> Jane Goodall believes in speaking out against the hunting and killing of wild chimps for food. She supports **protesting** the inhumane treatment of chimpanzees in medical laboratories.

Protesting means _____

Look at the target words and phrases. Which ones are new to you? Circle them here and in the reading. Then read "The Mind of the Chimpanzee" again. Look at the context of each new word and phrase. Can you guess the meaning? Use the Guessing Strategy where possible.

Target Words and Phrases

infant (1)	implied (2)	pile (4)	the wild (7)
meaningful (1)	possess (2)	combine (5)	stretch (8)
out of sight (1)	bitterly (2)	puzzled (5)	analyzing (8)
protest (2)	controversy (2)	eventually (5)	

Using the Vocabulary

These sentences are about the reading. Complete them with the words and phrases in the box. Circle the words or phrases in the sentences that help you understand the meaning of the target words.

bitter	combined	controversy	eventually	imply	infant
out of sight	pile	possess	protest	puzzled	

1. Washoe is the name of a chimpanzee who was adopted by a human family when she was very small. She was an _____ when they got her.

2. The Gardners wanted to find out if Washoe (and other chimps) might _____ the intellectual ability to learn and use language.

3. After they had taught Washoe sign language, the Gardners designed an experiment to test her understanding. They asked her to get an apple that was in another room, _____. Washoe left the room, and came back with the apple.

4. Washoe could understand language. But could she use language to communicate? One day, Washoe _____ the people taking care of her when she invented her own sign, asking for a "rock berry." At first, no one could make sense of Washoe's sign, but _____ they figured out that she had invented a sign for a type of sweet nut.

5. Washoe _____ two signs that she knew, rock and berry, to make a new word.

6. Not everyone in the scientific community was happy about the news of Washoe's achievements with language. In fact, there was a lot of _____ against the work that the Gardners and others were doing.

7. Some scientists were not comfortable with the idea that chimps could learn a language. If that were true, it would suggest, or _____, that chimps might possess intellectual skills similar to those of humans.

8. There was a lot of disagreement among scientists. It was a scientific _____.

9. Scientists on both sides disagreed strongly with each other. They sometimes got into _____ arguments.

10. Fortunately, the controversy led to more research. In other experiments, chimps proved that they could perform complex tasks, such as separating one _____ of objects into a number of different categories.

DEVELOPING READING SKILLS

Understanding Major Points and Supporting Details

A Which of these sentences are major points and which are supporting details? Write MP (major point) or SD (supporting detail).

_MP_ **1.** The lives of wild chimpanzees are very complex.

_____ **2.** Chimpanzees recognize people that they haven't seen in years.

_____ **3.** Chimpanzees can learn how to communicate with humans.

_____ **4.** Chimps have been taught some of the signs of ASL.

_____ **5.** Chimps are artistically creative.

_____ **6.** Chimps have good memories.

_____ **7.** All chimps learn what their position in chimp society is.

_____ **8.** Laboratory chimps like to draw and paint, and they give names to their "artwork."

_____ **9.** Chimps understand the meaning of *more* and *less*.

_____ **10.** Chimps have some math skills.

B Complete the chart with the information from Exercise A. Write the details next to the major points they support.

Major point	Supporting detail(s)
The lives of wild chimpanzees are very complex.	

Understanding Main Ideas

Answer this question.

What is the main idea of "The Mind of the Chimpanzee"?

_____

_____

Summarizing

Use the information from the previous two exercises, Understanding Major Points and Supporting Details and Understanding Main Ideas, to write a summary of the reading. Do not copy—paraphrase.

EXPANDING VOCABULARY

Using the Vocabulary in New Contexts

These sentences use the target words and phrases in new contexts. Complete them with the words and phrases in the box.

bitter	combine	controversy	eventually	implying	infant
out of sight	pile	possess	protest	puzzles	

1. When she was an _____, her doctors discovered a problem with her auditory system. Now she's three years old and almost totally deaf.

2. You are very gifted, but I'm not sure if you _____ the characteristics that make someone a truly great musician.

3. In English, we have an expression "_____, out of mind." It means that when you do not see someone for a long time, you have a tendency to forget them.

4. Please put the dirt in a _____ in a corner of the garden.

5. The newspaper received over 10,000 letters of _____ against the war.

6. There is a big _____ over uniforms at that school. About half of the parents want their children to wear them, and the other half don't.

7. I understand why you're angry, but your _____ comments are not going to improve the situation.

8. To make that cake, first _____ the flour and sugar in a large bowl.

9. Your answer _____ me. I can't make sense out of it.

10. Are you _____ that he stole the money? If that's what you're trying to say, you'd better have some evidence to prove it.

11. We can wait. He'll come home _____.

Word Families

Study the chart. Then look at the sentences below and complete the paraphrases with the appropriate forms of the boldfaced words. Make sure that your paraphrases are grammatically correct and have the same meaning as the original sentence. You might need to add or take away words. Be careful; you will not use all the words.

Noun	Verb	Adjective
analysis	analyze	analytical
controversy		controversial
implication	imply	
possession	possess	possessive
puzzle	puzzle	puzzling/puzzled
the wild		wild

1. You didn't **analyze** the problem very well.

   Your ___*analysis*___ of the problem was not very good.

2. He is someone who likes to **analyze** everything.

   He is _____ individual.

3. There was a **controversy** over the President's decision.

   The president's decision was _____.

4. What are you **implying**?

   What is _____ of what you just said?

5. He lost everything he **possessed** in the fire.

   The fire destroyed _____.

6. Some children don't like to share their **possessions** with anyone else.

   They _____ of the things that belong to them.

7. His angry reaction **puzzled** me.

   I was _____ the angry way that he reacted.

   His anger was a _____ to me.

8. It is important to protect animals living in **the wild**.

   We should _____ animals.

Studying Word Grammar

Some adjectives become nouns when the definite article *the* is in front of them. Look at the examples.

   The lives of chimpanzees in **the wild** are not so simple.

   They taught an infant chimpanzee the language used by **the deaf**.

In these sentences, the adjectives *wild* and *deaf* are used as nouns. Nouns of this kind refer to an entire category, not just one individual. Certain adjectives describing nationalities can also be used in this way. Look at the example.

   The French are famous for their talented chefs.

Be careful. Only nationalities that have no plural form are used in this way. For example, we do not say *The American* to refer to the people of the United States. Rather, we use the plural noun with no article—*Americans* (not *the* Americans).

Talk with a partner. Discuss what the people below are famous for.

- The Spanish
- The Swiss
- The Chinese
- The Japanese
- The _____ (your idea)

PUTTING IT ALL TOGETHER

Discussion

Share your ideas in a small group.

1. As scientists discover more and more similarities between humans and animals, it may become difficult to define what distinguishes human beings from other animals. Make a list of the characteristics that you believe make us human. As you talk, try to use the vocabulary below. Each time someone uses a target word or phrase, put a check (✓) next to it.

analyze/analysis	controversy/controversial	eventually
imply/implication	intend/intention/intentional	meaningful
possess/possession	protest	puzzle/puzzled/puzzling
the wild/wild		

2. In paragraph 5 of the reading, the writer describes how some chimps that have been taught sign language create their own, very clever signs for everyday objects—for example, "green banana" (cucumber). Choose five everyday objects, and invent your own "signs" for them. Each sign should be made of two simple words. For example, the sign for a *pencil* could be "writing stick." When you finish, see if the students in other groups can guess what your "signs" mean.

Writing

Complete one or both of these writing topics. When you write, use at least five of the target words from the chapter. Underline the target words in your paper.

1. Do some research either in the library or on the Internet on Jane Goodall and her work. Write a one- to two-page report about her.

2. Write an essay describing the characteristics that you believe distinguish human beings from other animals. As you are writing, consider your answers to question 1 in the **Discussion** section above. You can use information from the readings in Chapters 13, 14, and 15 to support your ideas, but do not copy—paraphrase.

Wrap-up

REVIEWING READING SKILLS AND VOCABULARY

Read the text. Do not use a dictionary.

1   On September 28, 2003, a 300-pound gorilla named Little Joe escaped from a city zoo in the United States. During his escape, the 11-year-old gorilla attacked and injured a two-year-old girl and her babysitter. Fortunately, their injuries were not serious, and Little Joe was eventually captured by police and returned to the zoo. However, those who witnessed the incident will not soon forget it. Said Mark Matthews, a firefighter who lives close to the zoo, "I saw the gorilla sitting at the bus stop. Everybody was scared, including the police."

2   Rhonda Devance also spotted the gorilla, but she couldn't make sense out of what she was seeing. "I thought it was a person. I thought it was a guy with a big black jacket and a snorkel on."

3   John Dorris, who as a long-time police officer is fairly used to strange incidents, said, "I thought I'd seen it all in 18 years."

4   The structure where Little Joe lives was thought to be escape-proof, so zoo officials were puzzled at how easy it was for him to get out. However, they were not at all puzzled by the escape attempt itself. At eleven years old, Little Joe can be compared to a human teenager who has reached physical maturity but is still intellectually and emotionally immature. It is common for apes at that age to become restless and seek more freedom. Indeed, experts familiar with Little Joe say that overall, he is a perfectly normal, healthy ape.

5   Not surprisingly, Little Joe's brief taste of freedom has led to protest from those who believe that it is inhumane to keep wild animals in zoos.

Comprehension Check

Read these sentences. Circle T (true) , F (false), or ? (can't determine the answer from the reading). If you circle F, change the sentence to make it true.

1. Little Joe escaped from the zoo because zoo workers were not watching him closely enough.   T   F   ?

2. John Dorris was surprised when he saw the escaped gorilla.   T   F   ?

3. Little Joe's behavior is unusual.   T   F   ?

4. Little Joe got on a city bus.   T   F   ?

5. People who think it is morally wrong to keep animals   T   F   ?
   in zoos have used Little Joe's story to support their
   opinion.

Guessing Meaning from Context

Find the words in the reading, and match each word to its definition. Be careful. Two definitions will not be used.

Word	Definition
_____ 1. capture	**a.** try to find or get something
_____ 2. spot	**b.** something that people wear on their face in order to breathe under water
_____ 3. snorkel	**c.** notice or recognize something that is unusual or difficult to see
_____ 4. escape-proof	**d.** avoid something that you are afraid of
_____ 5. ape	**e.** a very large nose
_____ 6. restless	**f.** catch and keep someone or something
_____ 7. seek	**g.** not allowing someone or something to get out of somewhere
_____ 8. inhumane	**h.** unable to stop moving because you are impatient, anxious, or bored
	i. a large monkey without a tail or with a very short tail, such as a gorilla
	j. treating people or animals in a way that is unkind or cruel

Paraphrasing

Paraphrase these sentences from the text.

1. Rhonda Devance also spotted the gorilla, but she couldn't make sense out of what she was seeing.

   _____

   _____

2. The structure where Little Joe lives was thought to be escape-proof, so zoo officials were puzzled at how easy it was for Little Joe to get out.

   _____

   _____

3. However, they were not at all puzzled by the escape attempt itself.

   _____

   _____

EXPANDING VOCABULARY

Studying Collocations

Look at the sentence containing the target word **bitter.**

> The announcement of the government's decision to go to war led to **bitter** protest.

The word *bitter,* meaning extremely angry or unpleasant, is part of several collocations:

Complete the sentences with the correct collocation from the box.

bitter protest	bitter argument	bitter disappointment	bitter wind	bitter end

1. She had no hat or coat to protect her from the _____.

2. The two brothers haven't spoken to each other since they had a _____ over money.

3. The fact that Tom did not graduate from college was a _____ to his parents.

4. Despite the _____ of people living in the area, the city cut down all the trees to make room for a new parking lot.

5. The movie seemed endless, but we stayed until the _____.

Word Families

Look at this sentence.

> Please do not **unfasten** your seat belts until the plane has come to a complete stop.

You learned in Unit 3 that the prefix *un-* means "not." But when the prefix *un-* is added to a verb, for example **fasten**, it means more than just "not." It means that something has already been done. (It means that the seat belts are already fastened.) In other words, before you can **unfasten** something, you need to **fasten** it.

On a separate piece of paper, answer these questions in complete sentences. Use the boldfaced words.

1. When you get back home after a trip, do you **unpack** immediately, or do you wait until the next day?

2. Have you ever locked yourself out of your car or your house? How did you finally **unlock** the door and get in?

3. When you go away on a long trip, is it a good idea to **unplug** your electrical appliances (for example, your toaster, coffee maker, or computer)? Why or why not?

4. Have you ever done anything in your life that you would like to **undo** if you could?

PLAYING WITH WORDS

Complete the puzzle with words you studied in Chapters 13–15.

Across

2. A group of animals or plants of the same kind that can breed with each other

4. Having an empty space inside

5. To develop by gradually changing or to make something do this

6. To join together the two sides of something so that it is closed

7. A very intelligent small African ape

8. A cover for a pot, box, or container

9. A baby

10. Confused and unable to understand something

Down

1. A scientist who studies living things

2. A series of musical notes that have a fixed order and become gradually higher or lower in pitch

3. A magazine or newspaper for people who are interested in a particular subject

5. Facts, objects, or signs that make you believe that something exists or is true

10. A large group of similar things collected or thrown together

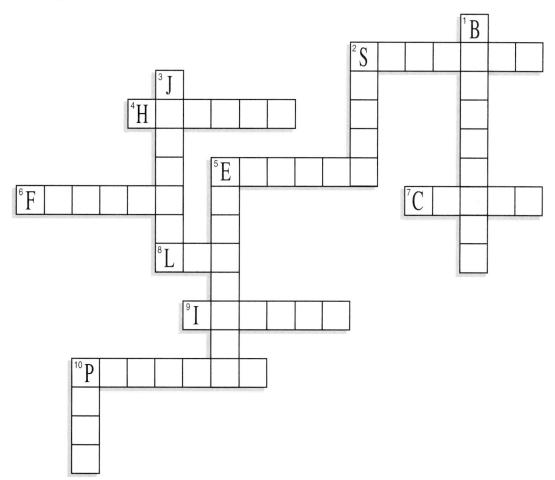

BUILDING DICTIONARY SKILLS

Finding the Correct Meaning

Many words have more than one meaning. Look at the dictionary entries below. Read each sentence and write the number of the meaning.

1.

> **bit·ter** /ˈbɪtɚ/ *adj* **1** very angry because you feel something bad or unfair has happened to you: *Kyle's bitter voice showed how upset he was.* **2** having a strong taste, like coffee without sugar **3** air that is bitter is cold and unpleasant: *a bitter wind* -see usage note at TEMPERATURE **4** **to/until the bitter end** until the end, even though unpleasant things happen: *The UN stayed in the war zone until the bitter end.* **-bitterly** *adv* **-bitterness** *n* [U]

   a. _____ He is **bitter** about losing his job.

   b. _____ This medicine has a **bitter** taste.

2.

> **wild¹** /waɪld/ *adj* **1** living or growing in a natural state, and not controlled by people: *wild horses* | *wild flowers* **2** showing strong uncontrolled emotions such as excitement, anger, or happiness: *a wild look in her eyes* | *wild applause from the audience* **3** SPOKEN exciting, interesting, unusual, or strange: *Sarah's party was really wild.* | *a wild haircut* | *"He's a year old and already saying words." "That's wild."* **4** done or said without knowing all the facts or thinking carefully about them: *Take a **wild guess.*** (=guess without thinking carefully) **5** **be wild about sth** SPOKEN to be very interested in or excited about something: *I'm not too wild about his movies.* **6** a wild card in a game can represent any card that you want it to be
> **wild²** *adv* **1** **run wild** to behave in an uncontrolled way because you have no rules or people to control you **2** **go wild** to suddenly become very noisy and active because you are excited or angry: *The crowd went wild when the Giants won.*
> **wild³** *n* **in the wild** in an area that is natural and not controlled or changed by people: *animals that live in the wild* -compare CAPTIVITY

   a. _____ I had a **wild** experience last night.

   b. _____ How can you make such a **wild** accusation? You have no proof!

   c. _____ I'm not **wild** about mushrooms. Please don't put any in my salad.

3.

> **stretch¹** /stretʃ/ *v* **1** [I,T] also **stretch out** to become bigger or looser as a result of being pulled, or to make something do this by pulling it: *Dad stretched my T-shirt!* | *My new sweater has stretched.* **2** [I,T] to reach out your arms, legs, or body to full length: *He **stretched** his arms **out** to try to reach the branch.* | *Be sure to stretch before you exercise.* **3** [I] to spread out over a large area, or continue for a long period: *The desert **stretched to** the horizon.* | *The project will probably **stretch into** next year*. **4** [I] if cloth stretches, it changes shape when you pull or wear it, and becomes its original shape when you stop: *The shorts stretch to fit your shape.* **5** [T] to pull something so it is tight: *We can stretch a rope between two trees.* **6 stretch sth to the limit** to use as much of a supply of something as is available, without having enough for anything else: *Our resources are already stretched to the limit.* **7 stretch your legs** INFORMAL to go for a walk
> **stretch out** *phr v* [I] INFORMAL to lie down so you can rest or sleep: *I'll just **stretch out** on the couch for a while.*
> **stretch²** *n* **1** an area of water or land: *a dangerous **stretch of** road* **2** a continuous period of time: *During the summer we worked 12 hours **at a stretch**.* (=without stopping) **3** the action of stretching part of your body **4** [U] the ability of a material to become bigger or longer without tearing **5 not by any stretch (of the imagination)** SPOKEN used in order to say that something is definitely not true: *She's not fat, by any stretch of the imagination.*

a. _____ My new jeans are a little tight, but they will **stretch**.

b. _____ Before you do any physical exercise, it's a good idea to **stretch**.

c. _____ I'm going to go out for a walk. I've been sitting all day.

I need to **stretch** my legs.

4.

> **scale¹** /skeɪl/ *n*
> **1 ▸ SIZE ◂** [singular, U] the size or level of something, when compared to what is normal: *a **large/small scale** project* | *They built their new house **on a grand scale**.* (=it is very big)
> **2 ▸ MEASURING SYSTEM ◂** [C usually singular] a system for measuring the force, speed, amount etc. of something, or for comparing it with something else: *a company's pay scale* | *On a scale from 1 to 10, I'd give it an 8.*
> **3 ▸ FOR WEIGHING ◂** [C usually plural] a machine or piece of equipment for weighing people or objects: *Here, put the bag of apples on the scales.*
> **4 ▸ MEASURING MARKS ◂** a set of marks with regular spaces between them on an instrument that is used for measuring: *a ruler with a metric scale*
> **5 ▸ MAP/DRAWING ◂** [C,U] the relationship between the size of a map, drawing, or model and the actual size of the place or thing that it represents: *a scale of 1 inch to the mile*
> **6 ▸ MUSIC ◂** a series of musical notes that have a fixed order and become gradually higher or lower in PITCH
> **7 ▸ ON FISH ◂** [C usually plural] one of the small flat pieces of hard skin that cover the bodies of fish, snakes etc.

a. _____ The doctor asked the patient to step on the **scale** so he could check her weight.

b. _____ Before you cook the fish, you must remove the **scales**.

c. _____ Please rate each essay on a **scale** from one to five, with one for the best one and five for the worst one.

UNIT 6

THE PEOPLE BEHIND THE SCIENCE

CHAPTER 16

A Woman's Fate

Dr. Jeong-Wha Choi and one of her inventions

GETTING READY TO READ

Ⓐ Talk with a partner or in a small group.

Based on the photograph and paragraph on page 212, imagine what the reading will be about, and write three questions you expect to be answered.

1. _____

2. _____

3. _____

B Read the first paragraph of "A Woman's Fate." Write the words or phrases that match the definitions below the paragraph.

The attractive, well-dressed woman holds up a pair of gloves. There seems to be nothing remarkable about them. But there's a story behind these gloves. It involves a war, a little girl who wanted to be a housewife, a determined mother, a talented student, three prestigious universities, and a unique ability to see the big picture.

Definition	Word or Phrase
1. Clothing worn on your hands, with separate parts to cover each finger	_____
2. Having a strong desire to continue to do something even when it is difficult	_____
3. Admired and respected as one of the best or most important	_____
4. Unusually good and special; the only one of its kind	_____
5. Look at a situation and understand the most important issues	_____

READING

Read the text once without stopping.

A Woman's Fate

1   The attractive, well-dressed woman holds up a pair of **gloves**. There seems to be nothing remarkable about them. But there is a story behind these gloves. It involves a war, a little girl who wanted to be a housewife, a **determined** mother, a talented student, three **prestigious** universities, and a **unique** ability to **see the big picture**.

2   Jeong-wha Choi was born in 1946 in Seoul, Korea. The only girl in a family of four children, Choi lost her father in the Korean War. Her mother went to work as a nurse to support her family. In Korea at that time, it was unusual for a woman to work outside the home, and as a child Choi was very sensitive to her mother's absence. Although an excellent student, she **resisted** her mother's attempts to interest her in a career in medicine. She knew exactly what she wanted to do with her life, and it did not involve medical school. Choi's dream was to be a stay-at-home wife and mother. Choi's mother, however, was determined that her children attend

continued

university. Choi agreed, but with one condition—she would not study medicine; she would study home economics.[1]

3   Choi entered prestigious Seoul National University, and did very well in her studies. Her professors encouraged her to go on to graduate school,[2] but with no intention of having a career, Choi was not interested. Fate, however, had different plans.

4   While Choi waited for a **suitable** husband to appear, she took a job with the government as a child welfare[3] worker. But after she had been at her job for only six months, one of her **former** professors offered her a job as an assistant to the department of Home Economics. It was an interesting opportunity, and she accepted.

5   Choi spent almost five years in the department. While she was there, she learned a lot about clothing and textiles.[4] Reading through international publications, she became fascinated by a field that did not even exist in South Korea at that time—clothing physiology. (Clothing physiology is the study of the biological **function**, or work, of clothing, specifically how clothing can contribute to or **interfere** with the healthy functioning of the human body.)

6   Although she had always dreamed of being a wife and mother, Choi accepted the fact that perhaps it was not her fate to marry. She therefore began to look for a graduate program where she could study clothing physiology. Japan seemed to be the best choice. She taught herself as much Japanese as she could by reading textbooks and looking through Japanese fashion magazines, and in January 1973, left South Korea for Japan.

7   Choi expected that it would be at least a year before she would be ready to take the university entrance exam. To her surprise, however, she passed after only two months of study. In March 1975, just two short years after her arrival in Japan, Choi graduated with a degree in clothing physiology from prestigious Nara Women's University. She then went on to get a Ph.D.[5] from the School of Medicine at Kobe University in Kobe, Japan.

8   As her research topic, Choi examined how Korean traditional clothing compares to western clothing in two ways: thermal adaptability (how well

continued

---

[1] *home economics* = the scientific study of the interaction of individuals, families, and communities with their work, social, and personal environments

[2] *graduate school* = a college or university where you can study for a master's degree or a Ph.D.

[3] *welfare* = the system by which the government provides money, free medical care, etc., for people who cannot provide for themselves

[4] a *textile* = any kind of cloth, including cloth that is made from natural or synthetic (=artificial) fabric, for example, a mechanically or chemically bonded fabric

[5] a *Ph.D.* = a doctorate degree from a university

the clothing allows the body to control temperature) and mobility (how well the clothing suits the wearer's movement). Choi's research **confirmed** that Korean traditional clothing, while beautiful, did not do very well on a physiological level.

9 In September 1979, Choi returned to Seoul National University, this time as an assistant professor in the same department where she had studied and worked years before. She has since done important research on the effects of clothing on the wearer's quality of life. She and her research team conduct scientifically controlled experiments to precisely measure the ways in which clothing affects mental, physical, and occupational[6] health and **well-being**. And that's what brings us back to those gloves.

10 As a scientist, one of Choi's strengths is her ability to notice problems that others do not, and then **come up with** solutions. On a visit to the South Korean countryside, Choi noticed the green **stains** and painful cracks on the farmers' hands. After analyzing the farmers' work habits and needs, she returned to her laboratory to design a glove suitable for their work. In coming up with the final design, Choi considered a range of factors, from **sweating** rate to worker productivity.[7] The gloves that she and her research team invented are made of a thin, light material that "breathes," making it comfortable enough for all-day wear. The fingers of the glove are covered in a material that stops the fingers from **slipping**. At the same time, the material is thin enough for the farmers to feel what they are doing. Choi and her research group have since patented[8] their invention, and their gloves are worn today by **agricultural** workers all over South Korea. The gloves have also begun to attract the attention of those in other professions, including pharmacists who find that the gloves are perfectly suited to their work.

11 Eventually, Choi did marry and have two children, but she is hardly a stay-at-home wife and mother. She lives in Seoul with her family and is a professor in the Department of Clothing and Textiles, College of Human Ecology,[9] at Seoul National University. She has published many papers in her field and has patents and patents pending[10] on a variety of inventions.

---

6 *occupational* = relating to a job

7 *worker productivity* = the rate at which goods are produced, and the amount produced

8 *patent* = get an official document that says that you have the right to make or sell a new invention and that no one else is allowed to do so

9 *ecology* = the scientific study of the way in which plants, animals, and people are related to each other and to their environment

10 *pending* = not yet decided, agreed on, or finished

Comprehension Check

Read these sentences. Circle T (true), F (false), or ? (can't determine the answer from the reading). If you circle F, change the sentence to make it true. Check your answers with a classmate. If your answers are different, look back at the reading.

1. When Choi was young, her mother did not live with her family.   T   F   ?
2. Choi was a better student than her brothers.   T   F   ?
3. Choi intended to work only until she got married.   T   F   ?
4. Choi decided to become a fashion designer.   T   F   ?
5. Choi spent two years learning Japanese.   T   F   ?
6. Choi wishes that she were a stay-at-home wife and mother.   T   F   ?

EXPLORING VOCABULARY

Thinking about the Vocabulary

Guessing Strategy

In Chapter 3, you learned that the signal word *or* can help you guess the meaning of unfamiliar words. Look at the example.

> Clothing physiology is the study of the biological **function**, or work, of clothing, specifically how clothing can contribute to or **interfere** with the healthy functioning of the human body.

Remember: The punctuation with the word *or* helps you guess meaning.

Try It!

Read the sentences, and write a definition of the **boldfaced** target words.

1. At her **former**, or previous, job she worked for the government.

   Former means _____

2. I couldn't decide whether to agree to his plan or **resist** it.

   Resist means _____

Look at the target words and phrases. Which ones are new to you? Circle them here and in the reading. Then read "A Woman's Fate" again. Look at the context of each new word and phrase. Can you guess the meaning? Use the Guessing Strategy where possible.

Target Words and Phrases			
fate (title)	see the big picture (1)	interfere (5)	stains (10)
gloves (1)	resisted (2)	confirmed (8)	sweating (10)
determined (1)	suitable (4)	well-being (9)	slipping (10)
prestigious (1)	former (4)	come up with (10)	agricultural (10)
unique (1)	function (5)		

Using the Vocabulary

These sentences are **about the reading**. Complete them with the words and phrases in the box. Circle the words or phrases in the sentences that help you understand the meanings of the target words.

agricultural	coming up with	confirm	fate	former	function
interfere	resisted	slip	stains	suitable	sweating
well-being					

1. As a child, Jeong-wha Choi decided that she would not have a career. However, it seems that being a housewife was not her _____.

2. When she was a young girl, Choi _____ her mother's attempts to interest her in a career in medicine. Instead, she wanted to study home economics.

3. A few months after Choi finished her studies at Seoul National University, one of her _____ professors offered her a job.

4. When Choi started her research on traditional clothing, she was not sure whether her results would _____ or disprove the theory that Korean traditional clothing was warmer than modern clothing.

5. Because Choi is interested in analyzing problems and _____ solutions, a career in science is especially _____ for her.

6. As a scientist, Choi wants to know if a particular type of clothing increases or decreases the wearer's health and comfort. She is interested in the clothing's effect on the physical and mental _____ of the wearer.

7. Some of Choi's projects involve Korean _____ workers, or farmers.

8. When Choi visited agricultural workers in Korea, she noticed the green _____ that they had on their hands from cutting plants.

9. When agricultural workers are cutting plants, they need to be able to hold the plants firmly so that the plants don't _____.

10. When Choi and her team designed gloves to help farmers in their work, they carefully considered the _____, or work, of the gloves.

11. She wanted her gloves to be comfortable for farmers to wear even in the hot sun. Therefore, she measured the farmers' _____ rate when they were wearing the gloves and when they weren't.

12. She did not want the gloves to _____ with the farmers' work. Rather, she wanted the gloves to make the farmers' work easier.

DEVELOPING READING SKILLS

Understanding Text Organization

To understand a reading that involves several different time periods, it is important to be able to put the important events into the correct time order.

Number the following events in the correct order. If you cannot determine from the reading when an event occurred, write a question mark (?).

_____ **a.** Choi graduated with a Ph.D.

__1__ **b.** The Korean War occurred.

_____ **c.** Choi studied home economics.

_____ **d.** Choi worked for six months as a child welfare worker.

_____ **e.** Choi learned Japanese.

_____ **f.** Choi discovered the field of clothing physiology.

_____ **g.** Choi's started working for her former professors.

_____ **h.** Choi conducted research on traditional Korean clothing.

_____ **i.** Choi became a professor at Seoul National University.

_____ **j.** Choi got married.

Recognizing Point of View

It is important to understand how a writer feels or think about a topic. Often, writers do not state their opinions, or points of view, directly. Rather, the reader needs to infer a writer's point of view.

Circle the statement that best expresses the writer's point of view.

1. The writer admires Jeong-wha Choi.
2. The writer thinks that all women should have careers.
3. The writer thinks that Jeong-wha Choi should not have had children.

Summarizing

Use the information from the previous two exercises, Understanding Text Organization and Recognizing Point of View, to write a summary of the reading. Do not copy—paraphrase.

EXPANDING VOCABULARY

Using the Vocabulary in New Contexts

These sentences use the target words and phrases in new contexts. Complete them with the words and phrases in the box.

agricultural	came up with	confirm	fate	former	function
interfere	resist	slip	stain	suitable	sweat
well-being					

1. I washed the shirt many times, but I couldn't get rid of the coffee _____.

2. That coat is not _____ for this cold weather. Why don't you buy a heavier one?

3. Be careful. The sidewalk is icy. You could _____ and fall.

4. Please don't _____ in my personal life. I can solve my own problems.

5. I know that I shouldn't eat ice cream because I'm on a diet, but I can't _____.

6. I made less money at my _____ job than at the job I have now.

7. It wasn't your fault. There was nothing you could do. It was _____.

8. Good doctors care about the _____ of their patients.

9. Please _____ your reservation by calling the airline 24 hours before departure.

10. The economy of that country is based on _____ products, particularly coffee, rice, and fruit.

11. It took them a long time, but eventually they _____ a name for their company.

12. I don't understand your _____ here. What exactly do you do?

13. I _____ a lot when it's hot.

Word Families

The prefix *inter-* means "between." Look at the sentence.

> I don't think you should **interfere** in their argument. You will only make things worse.

In this sentence, the word *interfere* means "come between."

Complete the sentences with the words below.

| interlocking | interaction | interpersonal | interstate | interrelated |

1. That company has offices in both New York and California so they have to pay _____ taxes.

2. In a puzzle, you must put together the _____ pieces.

3. This job calls for excellent _____ skills. If you have trouble getting along with others, this is not the right job for you.

4. Research has confirmed that the more _____ there is between teachers and students, the more the students learn.

5. Those two fields are _____. What happens in one field always affects the other.

Studying Phrasal Verbs

The phrasal verb **come up with** means "to think of an idea, plan, reply, etc." There are many phrasal verbs that are formed with the verb *come*.

Read the sentences. Think about the meaning of the boldfaced phrasal verbs. Then write answers to the questions.

a. The project was going well until last week. We **came up against** some unexpected problems.

b. They were best friends until that woman **came between** them.

c. I don't feel very well. I think I'm **coming down with** a cold.

d. I **came across** an article in the newspaper that I thought might interest you.

e. At my university, the professors **come down on** students who cheat.

1. What difficulties have you **come up against** in learning English?

   _____

   _____

2. Has anything or anyone ever **come between** you and your best friend? Explain.

   _____

   _____

3. What is the best thing to do if you feel that you are **coming down with** a cold or other illness?

   _____

   _____

4. When you are reading and **come across** a word that you are unfamiliar with, what should you do?

   _____

   _____

5. Do you think your parents should **come down** on their children if they don't do well in school? Why or why not?

   _____

   _____

PUTTING IT ALL TOGETHER

Discussion

Share your ideas in a small group. As you talk, try to use the vocabulary below. Each time someone uses a target word or phrase, put a check (✓) next to it.

come up with	confirm	former	function
suitable	unique	well-being	

Come up with an invention that will be useful in everyday life. When you are ready, present your invention to the class. Explain the problem that the invention solves, as well as the way that it functions. Be prepared to answer questions from the class.

Writing

Complete one or both of these writing topics. When you write, use at least five of the target words from the chapter. Underline the target words in your paper.

1. Imagine that you want to convince someone to produce the invention that you and your group have come up with. Write a letter to possible investors (people who might give you money to produce the invention). Your letter should include the following information:

   • What the invention was designed for

   • Who the invention was designed for

   • How the invention functions

   • Why people will want to buy this invention

2. What was the most important invention of the past 100 years? Write an essay describing the invention, who invented it, and why it was so significant. If you get information for your report from the Internet or the library, give your teacher a list of the Web sites, articles, and books that you used in your research. Write the report in your own words. Don't copy—paraphrase.

CHAPTER 17

The Father of Vaccination

Edward Jenner (1749–1823) vaccinates his son.

GETTING READY TO READ

 Talk in a small group or with the whole class.

1. Put a check (✓) next to the diseases that you are familiar with. If you are not familiar with one of the diseases, ask your classmates or look it up in your dictionary.

   _____ influenza (flu)   _____ smallpox   _____ chickenpox

   _____ HIV (AIDS)   _____ cancer   _____ malaria

2. For some diseases, your doctor can give you an injection[1] that will protect you from the disease. This injection is called a *vaccination*. Which of the diseases above can be prevented with a vaccination? Circle them. When you finish, check your answers with your teacher.

---

[1] an *injection* = the act of giving a drug by using a special needle

B The **boldfaced** words in the sentences below appear in the reading. Which words are new to you? Circle them. Then, read the sentences about the reading. Decide whether the pairs of words after each sentence have similar or different meanings. Write S (similar) or D (different).

1. Edward Jenner studied medicine in London because he wanted to become a **physician**.

    _____ physician / doctor

2. In the eighteenth century, physicians were trained in **surgery** so that they could operate on their patients.

    _____ surgery / operation

3. In those days, smallpox was a deadly disease. However, some people were fortunate, and got only a **mild** form of the disease.

    _____ mild / severe

4. Some people would **deliberately** attempt to get a mild form of the disease, so that later they wouldn't get a more severe case.

    _____ deliberately / intentionally

5. When Jenner started his experiments on smallpox, many other physicians criticized him. However, Jenner **ignored** the criticism, and continued his work.

    _____ ignored / paid attention to

READING

Read the text once without stopping.

The Father of Vaccination

1   In a small town in England in the middle of the eighteenth century, an eight-year-old boy named Edward Jenner was intentionally **infected** with a deadly disease. He was then locked in a barn[2] with other children who had been similarly infected. There they remained until they either died or recovered. Fortunately for humanity, Jenner survived.

2   Child **abuse**? No—variolation. A common **practice** in the eighteenth century, variolation involved **deliberately** infecting a healthy person with smallpox, a highly **contagious** disease that killed one in three infants and young children. It was believed that healthy people infected with the pus[3]

continued

---

[2] a *barn* = a large farm building in which animals are kept
[3] *pus* = a thick yellowish liquid produced in an infected part of the body

of patients sick with **mild** cases of smallpox would develop only a mild form of the disease. Those individuals would then be protected from smallpox for the rest of their lives. Although variolation was the only effective **means** of fighting smallpox at that time, it was quite dangerous. About 10 percent of those variolated came down with a severe case of smallpox.

3   Edward Jenner would never forget his terrible days in the barn. Perhaps that was what led him to choose medicine as a career. In 1761, at just 13, Jenner began his medical studies. By 1770, he was studying anatomy[4] and **surgery** under John Hunter at St. George's Hospital in London. With Hunter, Jenner was trained in the scientific method, which his instructor described simply as "Why think; why not try the experiment?"

4   After two years in London, Jenner returned to his hometown. He was a popular doctor, due to his gentle personality and surgical skill. One common **request** was for variolation. Jenner performed the **procedure** many times, although he used a less severe method than the one that he had suffered through as a child. Jenner observed that some of his variolated patients never developed even a mild case of smallpox. Because of his training in the scientific method, he wanted to understand why these particular individuals were able to resist the disease. He discovered that they had all previously had cowpox, a mild illness passed from cows to humans. Cowpox affected mostly people who worked closely with cows. Jenner observed that cowpox, while much less severe than smallpox, was in many ways similar to it. He was also aware of a traditional belief that people who had had cowpox never got smallpox. Based on his observations, Jenner came up with a theory. He believed that cowpox not only protected against smallpox, but could be passed from one human being to another as a deliberate means of protection.

5   In May 1796, Jenner finally got the chance to test his theory. He learned that a young woman from a local farm, Sarah Nelmes, had cowpox. Jenner asked the parents of an eight-year-old boy named James Phipps for **permission** to conduct a risky experiment on their son. Jenner chose James because he had never had cowpox or smallpox. Jenner removed pus from Sarah's hand and spread it on scratches he had made on the boy's arms. As expected, the boy developed a mild case of cowpox, but recovered rapidly. Jenner was now ready for the second, much riskier stage of his experiment. On July 1, 1796, Jenner variolated Phipps with pus from a smallpox patient. Jenner and other scientists and **physicians** waited anxiously for the results. Some were excited about Jenner's experiment, but many others accused him of taking too great a risk.

continued

---

[4] *anatomy* = the scientific study of the structure of human or animal bodies

6   In fact, James Phipps never developed smallpox. This was clear evidence to support Jenner's theory, but more data were needed. Jenner experimented successfully on 13 more patients, and at the end of 1796 wrote a report describing his work for the Royal Society.[5] However, it was **turned down** for publication. According to those who **reviewed** it, Jenner's theory was too much of a challenge to the accepted medical beliefs of the time.

7   Jenner **ignored** the criticism and continued experimenting. In 1798 he published his own book based on 23 cases in which vaccination (named for the *vaccinnia* virus[6] of cowpox) resulted in lasting protection against, or immunity to, smallpox. Although many people continued to criticize Jenner, some well-known London physicians were starting to vaccinate their patients. By the beginning of the nineteenth century, the practice of vaccination had spread throughout the world.

8   Eventually, Jenner's contributions to science were formally recognized. However, he never made an attempt to get rich through his discovery. Instead, he spent much of his time working, without pay, to spread the good news about vaccination. In 1977, the last known victim of smallpox recovered. No new cases appeared, and in 1980, the World Health Assembly announced that "the world and its peoples" were **free of** smallpox.

---

[5] the *Royal Society* = a group of respected physicians and scientists in London who review the research of other scientists

[6] a *virus* = a very small living thing that causes diseases that can be passed from one person or animal to another

Comprehension Check

Read these sentences. Circle T (true), F (false) or ? (can't determine the answer from the reading). If you circle F, change the sentence to make it true. Check your answers with a classmate. If your answers are different, look back at the reading.

1. When Edward Jenner was a boy, he got smallpox.   T   F   ?

2. Jenner decided to become a doctor because of his terrible   T   F   ?
   experience with smallpox as a child.

3. Because of his early experiences, Jenner refused to variolate   T   F   ?
   his patients.

4. Jenner discovered a cure for smallpox.   T   F   ?

5. At first, Jenner's work on vaccination was not accepted by   T   F   ?
the medical community.

6. The only reason Jenner's work is important is because it   T   F   ?
led to the elimination of smallpox.

EXPLORING VOCABULARY

Thinking about the Vocabulary

Guessing Strategy

The signal word *but* shows that a writer is contrasting two words or ideas. If you
understand the contrast the writer is making, it can help you guess the meaning of
unfamiliar words. Look at the example.

> Children who had a **mild** form of the disease usually survived, but those
> with a severe case almost always died.

In this sentence, the contrast is between a mild form of the disease and a *severe*
case. In Chapter 9 you learned that *severe* means "very serious." From this sentence,
you can see that *mild* is the antonym of *severe*. Therefore, *mild* means "not serious."

Try It!

Read the sentence, and write a definition of the **boldfaced** target word.

> That journal often accepts articles from well-known writers, but they **turned
> down** his paper because he has never published anything before.

Turn down means _____

**Look at the target words and phrases. Which ones are new to you? Circle
them here and in the reading. Then read "The Father of Vaccination"
again. Look at the context of each new word and phrase. Can you guess
the meaning? Use the Guessing Strategy where possible.**

Target Words and Phrases

vaccination (title)	**contagious** (2)	**request** (4)	**turned down** (6)
infected (1)	**mild** (2)	**procedure** (4)	**reviewed** (6)
abuse (2)	**means** (2)	**permission** (5)	**ignored** (7)
practice (2)	**surgery** (3)	**physicians** (5)	**free of** (8)
deliberately (2)			

Using the Vocabulary

These sentences are **about the reading**. Complete them with the words and phrases in the box. Circle the words or phrases in the sentences that help you understand the meanings of the target words.

abuse	contagious	free of	infected	means	permission
practice	procedure	request	reviewing	turned down	vaccination

1. Before Edward Jenner made his discovery, it was common medical _____ for doctors to deliberately infect children with a mild case of smallpox.

2. The doctors who infected the children with smallpox did not intend to _____ them. They were trying to protect them from developing a severe case of the disease.

3. Although they knew it was risky, parents requested the practice because at that time it was the only _____, or way, to protect their children from coming down with a more severe case of the deadly disease.

4. The _____, called variolation, involved putting a child into contact with a person who was infected with a mild case of the disease.

5. Because smallpox is a _____ disease, most children who had contact with someone suffering from smallpox would get sick.

6. However, not all children who were _____ with smallpox died. Those who got a mild form of the disease often recovered.

7. When physician Edward Jenner asked the Phipps family if he could use their son in an experiment, it was just a _____. They did not have to agree to it, but they did. They gave Jenner _____ to conduct the experiment.

8. As a result of those early experiments, Jenner eventually developed a medical procedure called _____.

9. However, Jenner's discovery was not immediately accepted. Indeed, when Jenner attempted to publish his research, he was _____ by the prestigious medical journals.

10. The Royal Society didn't do a good job of _____ Jenner's research. They just looked at it quickly and decided that his ideas were too new.

11. Fortunately, Jenner continued his research. Today, due to his work, the world is _____ the deadly disease of smallpox.

DEVELOPING READING SKILLS

Understanding Reference Words

In Chapter 11 you learned that a reference word takes the place of a noun or noun phrase. Reference words are often pronouns, such as *he, she,* and *it,* but in fact, almost any word can be a reference word. Look at the **boldfaced** words in the sentences.

> Jenner observed that some of the variolated patients never developed even a mild case of smallpox. Because of his training in the scientific method, he wanted to understand why **these particular individuals** were able to resist **the disease.**

In these sentences, the boldfaced words replace, or refer back to, something already mentioned in the text. The noun phrase *these particular individuals* refers back to *Jenner's variolated patients,* and *the disease* refers back to *smallpox.*

What do the boldfaced words refer to? Look back at the reading, and write your answers.

1. He was then locked in a barn with other children who had been similarly infected. **There** they remained until they either died or recovered. (paragraph 1)

   There = _____

2. With Hunter, Jenner was trained in the scientific method, **which his instructor** described simply as "Why think; why not try the experiment?" (paragraph 3)

   which = _____

   his instructor = _____

3. Jenner performed the procedure many times, although he used a less severe method than **the one** that he had suffered through as a child. (paragraph 4)

   The one = _____

4. In fact, James Phipps never developed smallpox. **This** was clear evidence to support Jenner's theory, but more data were needed. (paragraph 6)

   This = _____

5. However, he [Jenner] never made an attempt to get rich through **his discovery**. (paragraph 8)

   his discovery = _____

Understanding Main Points and Important Details

Complete the chart with information from the reading. If the reading does not contain the information, write a question mark (?). The completed chart should tell the story of Edward Jenner's life and work.

When?	What?	Where?	Who?
When Jenner was 8 years old			
		St. George's Hospital in London	
1772–May 1796			
May–July 1796			
End of 1796			The Royal Society
1797–1798			
1798			
1798–beginning of the nineteenth century			
1977			
	Announced that the disease of smallpox had been eliminated	?	World Health Assembly

Summarizing

Use the information in the chart as a guide to write a summary of the reading. Do not look back at the reading when you write your summary.

EXPANDING VOCABULARY

Using the Vocabulary in New Contexts

These sentences use the target words and phrases **in new contexts**. Complete them with the words in the box.

abuse	contagious	free of	infected	means	permission
practice	procedure	request	reviewed	turned down	vaccinations

1. His boss turned down his _____ for a pay increase.

2. For the well-being of the hospital staff, patients suffering from _____ diseases must be identified immediately and kept in a separate area.

3. The writer who _____ the movie was very critical.

4. I asked my boss for _____ to leave early.

5. We don't have the _____ to pay for a prestigious university for our son.

6. He was _____ for the job because his experience wasn't suitable.

7. Everyone should have a childhood _____ abuse.

8. That cut on your hand is _____. It's not getting better. You should ask a physician to look at it.

9. Could you please explain the _____ for getting a driver's license?

10. Before traveling to another country, your physician must confirm that you have received all of the required _____.

11. The police have evidence that her severe injuries were intentional. They are due to deliberate _____.

12. It is not my usual _____ to interfere in domestic arguments.

Word Families

Some words contain both a root and a prefix. For example, the target word **procedure** contains the root *ced*, which means "go" or "move," as well as the prefix *pro-*, which means "according to." The definition of a *procedure* is "something that follows a set of rules"—in other words, something that goes or moves forward according to certain rules.

Read the sentences. Using both context and what you know about the meaning of the root *ced* and the prefixes *inter-* (between or among), *pre-* (before) and *re-* (back or again), write a definition of each boldfaced word. Then, compare your definitions with a partner's. When you are finished, look the words up in your dictionary.

1. If the parents cannot agree on whether or not their daughter should have surgery, her physician will have to **intercede**.

   intercede: _____

2. As we drove away from the coast, the sound of the ocean **receded**.

   recede: _____

3. Variolation, a dangerous medical procedure, **preceded** the far safer practice of vaccination.

   precede: _____

Studying Collocations

The adjective **mild** and its antonym **severe** are used in several common collocations.

Read the sentences. Think about the meaning of the boldfaced collocations. Then write answers to the questions. Use complete sentences.

a. There is going to be a **severe storm** tomorrow. If you can, stay at home.

b. My husband is very **mild-mannered**. He almost never gets angry.

c. Most American food has a very **mild taste**. I prefer food with a stronger flavor.

d. Don't worry. You just have a **mild cold**.

e. When the president announced his plan to raise taxes, he came up against **severe criticism**.

f. He's in such **severe pain** that he can't walk.

g. After the dentist removes the tooth, you might experience some **mild pain**.

1. What is the most **severe** storm you have ever experienced? Describe it.

   _____

   _____

2. How does a **mild-mannered** person behave?

   _____

   _____

3. Do you prefer food with a **mild** taste or a spicy taste?

   _____

   _____

4. Have you ever had a **mild** case of a serious disease? Explain.

   _____

   _____

5. Have you ever experienced **severe** criticism for something you've done? Explain.

   _____

   _____

6. What can you do to deal with **mild** pain? **Severe** pain?

   _____

   _____

PUTTING IT ALL TOGETHER

Discussion

Share your ideas in a small group. As you talk, try to use the vocabulary below. Each time someone uses a target word or phrase, put a check (✓) next to it.

abuse	contagious	deliberately	free of
infect	means	mild	permission
physician	practice	procedure	request
surgery	turn down	vaccination/vaccine	

1. One problem with testing new vaccines is that it is risky to use an untested vaccine on human beings. Today, there are laws that limit scientists' ability to conduct such experiments. However, those laws did not exist in Edward Jenner's time. Discuss the advantages and disadvantages of laws that limit scientists from conducting experiments on human beings. Under what

circumstances is it acceptable to allow experiments on humans? Under what circumstances is it unacceptable?

2. What medical advances do you think will occur in your lifetime? Consider the following questions in your discussion: Which diseases will be cured? For which diseases will a vaccine be developed? Will life expectancy (how many years a human being, on average, lives) increase? By how many years?

Writing

Complete one or both of these writing topics. When you write, use at least five of the target words from the chapter. Underline the target words in your paper.

1. Conduct research either in the library or on the Internet on vaccines that scientists are currently working to develop. Write a report on your findings. Write the report in your own words. Do not copy—paraphrase. Give your teacher a list of the Web sites, articles, and books that you used in your research.

2. Write an essay based on question 1 in the **Discussion** section above.

CHAPTER 18

A Nose for Science

Luca Turin

GETTING READY TO READ

A Talk with a partner or in a small group.

1. Do you like to wear cologne?[1] If so, do you always wear the same kind, or do you change what you are wearing depending on the situation? Are there any situations for which wearing cologne is not appropriate? Explain.

2. Which sense is the most important to you—sight, hearing, speech, touch, taste, or smell? The least? Why?

---

[1] *cologne* = a liquid that smells slightly like flowers or plants, which you put on your neck and wrists

B Read the paragraph and answer the questions.

One of France's most famous royal couples was King Louis the XVI and his wife, Marie Antoinette. There are many stories about Marie Antoinette, but one tale is especially interesting. It involves her attempted escape from Paris during the French Revolution. According to the legend, Marie Antoinette and Louis XVI dressed in the clothes of simple travelers in order to escape from France. However, although Marie Antoinette's clothing was simple, her fragrance was not. Marie Antoinette and her husband were caught when someone smelled the expensive perfume that she was wearing. They knew that she was not an ordinary person, because only a member of royalty could afford such an expensive scent.

1. What are the three nouns in the paragraph that refer to **smells**?

   _____, _____, _____

2. What are the two nouns in the paragraph that refer to a type of story?

   _____, _____

3. What is the adjective in the paragraph that means "relating to or belonging to a king or queen"? _____

4. What is the noun form of the adjective in question 3? _____

READING

Read the text once without stopping.

A Nose for Science

1   In 1791, Marie Antoinette[2] escaped Paris with her husband, Louis XVI. Dressed as simple travelers, they left for Austria. But before they arrived, they were caught. How? The **legend** says that when the queen stepped down from her carriage[3] in a cloud of expensive **perfume**, everyone knew she must be **royalty**. No ordinary person could afford to wear anything that smelled so heavenly. The queen eventually paid for the mistake with her life.

2   This is just one of the many perfume **tales** that scientist Luca Turin enjoys retelling. Turin is a biophysicist[4] with an unusual hobby—collecting

continued

_____

[2] *Marie Antoinette* = wife of Louis XVI, the king of France from 1774–1792. They were both put in jail and killed during the French Revolution.

[3] a *carriage* = a vehicle with wheels that is pulled by a horse, used in past times

[4] a *biophysicist* = a scientist who studies the natural forces that affect living things

perfume. And as unlikely as it might seem, Turin's hobby has led him to develop a scientific theory that could win him a Nobel Prize[5]—or at least make him very rich.

3   Turin has been **obsessed** by smell since he was a boy and he used to **entertain** himself by analyzing the **scents** of wild plants. He has an unusually sensitive nose and is very good at identifying different scents. Turin describes his excellent sense of smell in this way: "Every perfume I've ever smelled has been to me like a movie, sound and vision . . .. To me, smell is just as real as they are." When he was a young scientific researcher in Nice, France, Turin frequently visited local perfume shops, collecting rare **fragrances**. He was well-known for his ability to smell a perfume and analyze it, immediately identifying the individual scents that it contained.

4   As he added to his perfume collection, Turin was also progressing in his scientific career. Although trained as a biologist, he considered the division of science into separate fields—biology, chemistry and **physics**—to be artificial. He moved freely from one field to another, following a **path** determined only by his interest and intellect. In that way, he gained a wider range of knowledge than most scientists possess.

5   At the same time, Turin's fascination with perfume grew. One day he and some friends visited a large **discount** perfume store where Turin bought almost everything on the shelves. On the way home, he entertained his friends by describing the fragrances in language that was so **poetic** that they told him he should write a book.

6   He decided to do exactly that. In 1992, Turin's book was published as *Parfums: Le Guide* (*Perfume: The Guide*). In it, Turin skillfully critiques some of the world's most famous fragrances. For example, this is how he describes *Rush,* by Gucci: "It smells like an infant's breath mixed with his mother's hair spray[6]. . . What *Rush* can do, as all great art does, is create a yearning,[7] then fill it with false memories of an invented past . . . ."

7   Turin's book caused a sensation among the **secretive** "Big Boys"—the seven large companies that control the world scent market. Turin's talent at translating smell into words won him a rare invitation to visit their laboratories. There, Turin discovered that the widely accepted theory about

continued

---

[5] a *Nobel Prize* = a prize given in Sweden each year to people from any country for important work in science, literature, economics or work toward world peace

[6] *hair spray* = a sticky liquid that is forced out of a special container in a stream of very small drops and that you put on your hair to make it stay in place

[7] a *yearning* = a strong desire or feeling of wanting something

how we are able to identify particular smells—by the shape of their molecules[8]—did not seem to work. Under this theory, it should be fairly easy for a chemist to "build" new molecules and accurately predict what they will smell like. But in fact, this is not the case. Each new smell the Big Boys create involves an **investment** of millions of dollars. That is because only a very small percentage of the new molecules possess the desired fragrance.

8   Now Turin had a new obsession: solving the mystery of smell. As a scientist with an extremely sensitive nose, an obsession with perfume, **access** to the Big Boys' laboratories, and a wide range of scientific knowledge, he was particularly well-suited to the challenge. Within just three years, Turin believed that he had the answer. The key was not the shape of the molecules, but rather their vibrations.[9]

9   Turin sent a paper presenting his theory to the prestigious science journal *Nature,* and waited anxiously for a response. However, a few scientific reviewers recommended that *Nature* turn the paper down. (It was eventually published in the journal *Chemical Senses.*) Scientists who had based their careers on the old theory of smell also reacted negatively, and he was even accused of **fraud**.

10   Turin's explanation? He is sharply critical of the **standards** for publication in science journals. He argues that the reviewers turned his paper down due to their narrow **focus** on just one field of science. Therefore, they couldn't make sense out of a complex theory involving biology, chemistry, and physics.

11   Luca Turin has since started his own company, Flexitral, where he uses his theory to create scent molecules to sell to the Big Boys. And like all scientists with controversial ideas, he waits for the day when his achievements will be properly recognized.

---

[8] a *molecule* = the smallest unit into which any substance can be divided without losing its own chemical nature

[9] a *vibration* = a continuous, small, shaking movement

Comprehension Check

Read these sentences. Circle T (true), F (false) or ? (can't determine the answer from the reading). If you circle F, change the sentence to make it true. Check your answers with a classmate. If your answers are different, look back at the reading.

1. Turin's interest in smell led him to become a scientist.　　T　　F　　?

2. Turin wrote a scientific book about perfume.　　T　　F　　?

3. Turin came up with a new theory about how we are able to distinguish different scents.　　T　　F　　?

4. Turin's theory is widely accepted within the scientific community.　　T　　F　　?

5. Turin thinks that the scientists who reviewed his theory did not treat him or his theory fairly.　　T　　F　　?

6. Turin will receive a Nobel Prize.　　T　　F　　?

EXPLORING VOCABULARY

Thinking about the Vocabulary

Guessing Strategy

Words that express cause-and-effect relationships can help you guess the meaning of unfamiliar words or phrases. Look at the example.

> He described the fragrances in language that was so **poetic** that they told him he should write a book.

In this sentence, the cause-and-effect relationship expressed by *so . . . that* indicates that poetic language is good enough to be in a book, so you can infer that it is well-written. The exact definition of *poetic* is "graceful, beautiful, and having deep feelings."

Try It!

Read the sentence, and write a definition of the **boldfaced** target word.

> Turin was so **obsessed** with coming up with a theory of smell that he couldn't think of anything else.

Obsessed means _____

Look at the target words. Which words are new to you? Circle them here and in the reading. Then read "A Nose for Science" again. Look at the context of each new word. Can you guess the meaning? Use the Guessing Strategy where possible.

Target Words

legend (1)	entertain (3)	discount (5)	access (8)
perfume (1)	scents (3)	poetic (5)	fraud (9)
royalty (1)	fragrances (3)	secretive (7)	standards (10)
tales (2)	physics (4)	investment (7)	focus (10)
obsessed (3)	path (4)		

Using the Vocabulary

These sentences are **about the reading**. Complete them with the words in the box. Circle the words or phrases in the sentences that help you understand the meanings of the target words.

access	discount	entertaining	focused	fraud	investment
obsessed	path	physics	poetic	secretive	standards

1. Scientist Luca Turin enjoys _____ people with interesting stories about perfume.

2. Turin is fascinated by different scents. In fact, you could say that he is _____ with smell.

3. One day, Turin went to a _____ perfume store. The prices were very low, and he bought almost every perfume there.

4. Turin is a scientist, but he is also a very artistic writer. His descriptions of perfume are remarkably _____.

5. The makers of expensive perfume are so _____ that they almost never let anyone visit their labs.

6. Turin was given _____ to the laboratories of the perfume makers because they were impressed by his perfume guide.

7. Turin has used his knowledge of science, particularly biology, chemistry, and _____, to come up with a scientific theory of how we are able to smell.

8. Turin follows a different _____ from others. He doesn't follow the way other people do things. He comes up with his own way.

9. Some scientists do not believe Turin's theory, and one has accused him of deliberately changing or inventing data—in other words, scientific _____.

10. Turin believes his paper was turned down because a small number of powerful scientists have too much of an _____ in the old theory of smell to admit that Turin's theory is correct.

11. According to Turin, the reviewers of his paper were so _____ on their individual fields of science that they couldn't see the big picture.

12. Turin hopes that by telling his story, he can help change the _____ that prestigious science journals use when they decide whether or not to publish a paper.

DEVELOPING READING SKILLS

Understanding Purpose

To understand a text, it is important to understand *why* the writer wrote the text, or the writer's **purpose**. When you read, try to answer these questions about the information in a text:

• Why did the writer include this particular information?
• Why did the writer present the information in this particular order or in this particular way?

Complete the sentences. Circle a or b.

1. The writer includes the legend about Marie Antoinette
   a. to teach the reader some French history.
   b. to get the reader interested in the text.

2. The writer includes the quote from Luca Turin in paragraph 3
   a. to help the reader understand why Turin is so interested in smell.
   b. to convince the reader that smell is an important sense.

3. The writer includes information about Turin's perfume guide because
   a. it shows that Turin has a very sensitive sense of smell.
   b. it shows what a talented writer Turin is.

4. The writer of the text believes
   a. that Turin's theory of smell could be correct.
   b. that Turin should not have challenged the scientific community.

Summarizing

Ⓐ Put a check (✓) next to the topics that should be included in a summary of the reading.

_____ a. the legend about Marie Antoinette's perfume

_____ b. Turin's visit to a discount perfume store

_____ c. Turin's perfume guide

_____ d. Turin's description of the fragrance *Rush*

_____ e. Turin's lifelong fascination with smell

_____ f. Turin's scientific background

_____ g. the shape theory of smell

_____ h. Turin's theory of smell

_____ i. *Nature*'s reaction to Turin's theory

_____ j. Turin's opinion about why his theory is not accepted by many scientists.

Ⓑ Use both Exercise A and your answers to **Understanding Purpose** to write a summary of the reading. Do not copy—paraphrase.

EXPANDING VOCABULARY

Using the Vocabulary in New Contexts

These sentences use the target words **in new contexts**. Complete them with the words in the box.

access	discount	entertain	focus	fraud	investment
obsessed	path	physics	poetic	secretive	standards

1. She is so _____ with detail that she can't see the big picture.

2. Originally, these gloves were priced at $100, but I got them at a 50 percent _____.

3. The academic _____ for entering a prestigious university are very high. Fortunately, I have excellent grades.

4. The reviewer said the movie was wonderful. He said it would _____ the whole family.

5. The former president of my company was accused of _____. The company lost a lot of money while he was president.

6. That business is a good _____. You will make a lot of money from it.

7. My _____ professor is the best scientist at the university.

8. _____ to that room is restricted. Only a few employees can enter.

9. Stay on the walking _____, and you won't get lost. It's easy to follow.

10. Don't worry about the details. Just _____ on the main ideas.

11. I don't understand why my son is suddenly so _____. What is he hiding?

12. You have such an original and _____ way of saying things. How did you learn to speak so beautifully?

Word Families

As you have seen in previous chapters, adjectives can have a variety of suffixes, such as *-ous, -ful, -ic, -al, -ed,* and *-ing.* Other adjective endings include the suffixes *-ive, -ent,* and *-ary.*

Complete the sentences with the adjectives below.

| fraudulent | legendary | obsessive | secretive |

1. There is no reason to be so _____. Everyone already knows what happened.

2. The _____ movie actor died yesterday at the age of 82.

3. I'm concerned about you. You are becoming _____ about your work. Don't be such a perfectionist!

4. He was arrested for possessing _____ identification papers.

Understanding Word Grammar

A **reflexive pronoun** is an object pronoun that is used when the subject and object of a verb are the same. Never use a reflexive pronoun if the subject and the object of the verb are different. Look at the examples.

Correct: He used to entertain **himself** by analyzing the scents of wild plants.	The reflexive pronoun *himself* is used **correctly** in this example because the subject and object of the verb are the same.
Incorrect: **His mother** entertained himself by telling him Greek legends.	The reflexive pronoun *himself* is used **incorrectly** in this example because the subject and object of the verb are different.

The reflexive pronouns in English are *myself, yourself, himself, herself, itself, themselves, yourselves, ourselves,* and *oneself.*

Answer these questions. Use the boldfaced verbs in your answers. Be careful. When you answer the questions, the pronouns may change.

1. What do you and your friends do to **entertain yourselves**? When your friends are busy, what do you do to **entertain yourself**?

   _____

   _____

2. Do you think teachers should try to **entertain their students**? Why or why not?

   _____

   _____

3. In which sports is it common for the players to **injure themselves**? Have you ever **injured yourself** when you were playing a sport? Have you ever **injured anyone else** when you were playing a sport? Explain what happened.

   _____

   _____

4. Are you someone who likes to **analyze yourself** and your behavior? Do you like it when other people try to **analyze you** and your behavior?

   _____

   _____

PUTTING IT ALL TOGETHER

Discussion

Share your ideas in a small group. As you talk, try to use the vocabulary below. Each time someone uses a target word or phrase, put a check (✓) next to it.

1. "A Nose for Science" is about a scientist who has come up with a new theory that is not generally accepted by the scientific community. Look at the list of scientists below. First, match the scientists to their theories or discoveries. Then, circle those whose ideas were not accepted at first by the scientific community but later were proven to be true. Talk about why their ideas weren't accepted at the time. Consider whether there were any powerful people or groups who argued against accepting their ideas. Finally, compare your answers to those of other groups.

access	focus	fraud/fraudulent	invest	legend/legendary
obsession/obsessive	physics	secretive	standard	

Scientist	**Theory or Discovery**
_____ Marie Curie	**a.** the theory of relativity
_____ Charles Darwin	**b.** the theory of gravity
_____ Albert Einstein	**c.** the theory of evolution
_____ Galileo Galilei	**d.** the discovery of the relationship between bacteria and disease
_____ Isaac Newton	**e.** the discovery of the elements radium and polonium
_____ Louis Pasteur	**f.** the discovery that planets orbit (turn around) the sun

2. How do the following things smell to you? Complete the chart individually. Then share your answers with your group. Did any of your classmates' answers surprise you?

	Wonderful	Good	Neutral	Bad	Disgusting
Freshly cut grass					
Horses					
Fresh fish					
Frying onions					
Leather					
A new car					
An infant					

Writing

Complete one or both of these writing topics. When you write, use at least five of the target words from the chapter. Underline the target words in your paper.

1. Choose one of the scientists your group discussed. Do some research on him or her in the library or on the Internet, and write a report. Include the following information in your report:

   • Background (nationality, education, family, etc.)

   • How he/she developed the theory or made the discovery

   • Research, experiments, etc., done to back up the theory or discovery

   • Scientific and public reaction to the theory or discovery

   • When and how the theory or discovery was finally accepted

   Write the report in your own words (don't copy—paraphrase). Give your teacher a list of the Web sites, articles, and books that you used in your research.

2. Think of a smell that you associate with a particular memory of a person, place, or situation. Write a description of the memory. Use specific details to make it come alive.

Wrap-up

REVIEWING READING SKILLS AND VOCABULARY

Read the text. Do not use a dictionary.

1   There is concern among some in the scientific community that fewer and fewer young people are choosing careers in science and technology. Studies of university students confirm that this reduction could soon lead to a shortage of new scientists. At a time when fascinating scientific discoveries seem to be occurring almost every day, how can this lack of interest be explained?

2   Experts who have reviewed the data believe that the key to the problem is in the way that science is taught. They claim that the teaching practices used in introductory science classes are suitable for only a small percentage of learners. For example, while most people are visual learners, most science professors use few visual images in their teaching. Instead, they present information verbally, either through written words and formulas, or spoken words in lectures. This leaves the visual learners in the class without the means to make sense of the information.

3   But what about laboratory classes? Aren't they perfectly suited to visual learners? Maybe, but there's a problem. In a standard physics lab, for example, students usually focus on detailed procedures, rather than the big picture. They are given an experiment to perform, but have little opportunity to analyze what they are doing and explore how it relates to the larger theory or to their everyday lives.

4   What can be done to make science teaching more meaningful to more students? Experts in science education believe that teachers need to focus on the educational well-being of all of the students in their classes. To that end, they should come up with methods and activities that will be effective for a variety of learners.

Comprehension Check

Read these sentences. Circle T (true), F (false), or ? (can't determine the answer from the reading). If you circle F, change the sentence to make it true.

1. Scientists are worried that students who graduate from universities with science degrees are not well-trained.   T   F   ?

2. The way that science is taught in schools is not effective for the majority of the students.   T   F   ?

3. Science teachers often use visual images that confuse their students.   T   F   ?

4. In most science lab classes, students have a chance to understand theories and relate them to their individual experiences.   T   F   ?

5. Overall, science teachers are not very interested in the well-being of their students.   T   F   ?

Guessing Meaning from Context

Find a word or phrase in the text that matches each of the definitions below. The numbers in parentheses are the paragraphs where you can find the word or phrase.

Definition	Word or Phrase
1. pictures that describe ideas (2)	_____
2. with words rather than pictures (2)	_____
3. a series of numbers or letters that represent a mathematical or scientific rule (2)	_____
4. for that purpose (4)	_____

Understanding Inference

Use inference to answer these questions.

1. Does the writer of the text imply that visual images are more important in the teaching of science than in other subjects? Explain.

   _____

   _____

   _____

2. Give two or more specific examples of visual images that science teachers could use in class to make science easier for visual learners.

   _____

   _____

   _____

Summarizing

Write a summary of the text. Remember, do not copy—paraphrase.

EXPANDING VOCABULARY

Studying Phrasal Verbs

In Chapter 17 you learned the phrasal verb **turn down.** There are many phrasal verbs that are formed with the verb **turn.**

Ⓐ **Read the sentences, and write the meaning of the boldfaced phrasal verbs.**

1. On the night the restaurant opened, there were so many customers that they had to **turn** people **away**.

   _____

   _____

2. Don't worry about him. He's always late. He'll **turn up** eventually.

   _____

   _____

3. Has anyone **turned in** a set of keys? I think I lost mine somewhere in the building.

   _____

   _____

4. You should be proud of your son. He's **turned into** a fine young man.

   _____

   _____

5. I liked my boss at first, but after a few weeks, his negative attitude **turned me off**.

   _____

   _____

Ⓑ **Answer these questions in complete sentences. Use the boldfaced phrasal verbs.**

1. When was the last time you were **turned away** from a restaurant or other public place?

   _____

   _____

   _____

2. What would you do if you were waiting for a friend and he never **turned up**?

   _____

   _____

   _____

3. If you found $100 in an empty classroom, would you **turn** it **in**? Why or why not?

_____

_____

_____

4. At what temperature does water **turn into** ice?

_____

_____

_____

5. What kinds of movies **turn** you **off**?

_____

_____

_____

Word Families

When you learn a new word, check to see if it contains a word part—a prefix, suffix, or root. Then, use your understanding of the meaning of the word to help you guess the meaning of the word part. The next time you see a word that contains that word part, it will be easier for you to guess its meaning.

A The words *physics* and *physician* both contain the root *phys*. The word *unique* contains the prefix *uni-*, and the word *agricultural* contains the prefix *agr-*. Use your understanding of the meanings of the words to write the meanings of the word parts.

1. The root *phys* means _____.

2. The prefix *uni-* means _____.

3. The prefix *agr-* means _____.

B Working with a partner, answer the questions. Make sure you use the **boldfaced** words in your answers.

1. How often do you go to your doctor for a **physical**?

2. What is a **unisex** bathroom? Are there **unisex** bathrooms in public places in your city?

3. Would you like to live in an **agrarian** community? Why or why not?

PLAYING WITH WORDS

Look back at the lists of target vocabulary on pages 216, 226, and 239. In a small group, write as many target words and phrases as you can under each category. Be ready to explain your answers. Some words might fit under more than one category, and some words might not fit under any category.

Success and failure	Health	Scientific research	Smell	Money
prestigious confirm		confirm		prestigious

BUILDING DICTIONARY SKILLS

Finding Idioms

An **idiom** is a group of two or more words that has a special meaning that is different from the ordinary meaning of the separate words. For example, the phrase *see the big picture* is an idiom. Most dictionaries do not have separate entries for idioms. Instead, they can be found under the entry for a key verb or noun in the idiom.

 Read the dictionary entries, and circle the idioms.

1.
> **pic·ture**[1] /ˈpɪktʃɚ/ *n*
> **1 ▸ IMAGE ◂** a painting, drawing, or photograph: *I have a **picture of** my family on the wall.* | ***Draw/paint a picture of** your house.* | *a group of tourists **taking pictures** (=taking photographs)* | *Leo's picture (=photograph of him) is in the newspaper.*
> **2 ▸ SITUATION ◂** [singular] the general situation in a place, organization etc.: *The **political picture** has greatly changed since March.*
> **3 ▸ DESCRIPTION ◂** [C usually singular] a description that gives you an idea of what something is like: *The report **paints a** clear **picture** of life in the army.*
> **4 be in/out of the picture** INFORMAL to be involved or not be involved in a situation: *With his main rival out of the picture, the mayor has a chance of winning the election.*
> **5 ▸ ON A SCREEN ◂** the image that you see on a television or in a movie: *Something's wrong with the picture.*
> **6 get the picture** SPOKEN to understand something: *I don't want you around here any more, get the picture?*
> **7 ▸ MOVIE ◂** OLD-FASHIONED ⇨ MOVIE: *Grandma loved going to the pictures.*

2.

> **means** /minz/ *n* [plural] **1** a method, system, object etc. that is used as a way of doing something: *We'll use any means we can to raise the money.* | *She took up photography as a means of earning a living.* | *The oil is transported by means of* (=using) *a pipeline.*
> **2 by all means** said in order to emphasize that someone should do or is allowed to do something: *By all means, drink while you are exercising.* **3 by no means** FORMAL not at all: *The results are by no means certain.* **4 a means to an end** something that you do or use only to achieve a result: *Bev always says her job is just a means to an end.* **5** the money or things that you have that make it possible for you to buy or do things: *They don't have the means to buy a car.* | *a man of means* (=who is rich)

3.

> **free¹** /fri/ *adj*
> **1 ▸ NOT RESTRICTED ◂** allowed to live, exist, or happen without being controlled or restricted: *People should be free to choose their own religion.* | *This is the country's first free election* (=not controlled by the government) *in 30 years.*
> **2 ▸ NO COST ◂** not costing any money: *I won free tickets for tonight's concert.*
> **3** not having any of a particular substance: *sugar-free bubble gum*
> **4 ▸ NOT BUSY ◂** not busy doing other things: *If you're free next weekend do you want to go see a movie?*
> **5 ▸ NOT BEING USED ◂** not being used at this time: *Excuse me, is this seat free?*
> **6 feel free** SPOKEN used in order to tell someone that s/he is allowed to do something: *Feel free to ask me any questions after the class.*
> **7 ▸ NOT A PRISONER ◂** not a prisoner or SLAVE: *The UN demanded that the three American hostages be set free.* (=be given their freedom)
> **8 free of/from sth** without something, especially something bad or unpleasant: *free of danger* | *free from disease*

B Complete each sentence with the correct idiom from the dictionary entries above.

1. If you have any problems, _____ to give me a call. I'll be happy to help you.

2. Now that his former girlfriend is _____, he is free to date someone else.

3. Some students study just because they enjoy it, but for many students, studying is _____.

Vocabulary Self-Test 2

Circle the letter of the word or phrase that best completes each sentence. Example:

She was seriously _____ in a car accident.

a. ignored   **c.** injured

b. bitter   **d.** ashamed

1. She is nine months _____. She will be having her baby any day now.

   a. innate   **c.** obvious

   b. out of sight   **d.** pregnant

2. When I moved to England, it took me a long time to _____ driving on the left side of the road.

   a. get used to   **c.** pull in front

   b. back up   **d.** make up for

3. How did you _____ your car? Did you have an accident?

   a. eliminate   **c.** possess

   b. fasten   **d.** damage

4. I have tried to _____ her behavior, but I just can't understand her.

   a. turn down   **c.** come up with

   b. recognize   **d.** make sense of

5. Put on your _____. It's cold outside.

   a. gloves   **c.** legends

   b. stains   **d.** perfume

6. I don't believe in _____. I think that with hard work, you can make anything happen.

   a. function   **c.** controversy

   b. fate   **d.** familiarity

7. You should never touch a _____ animal.

   a. socialized   **c.** wild

   b. puzzled   **d.** mild

8. If you want to drive, you need to buy car _____ in case you get into an accident.

    a. vehicle   **c.** discount

    b. insurance   **d.** permission

9. When his wife died, he never thought he would recover from his

    _____.

    a. grief   **c.** version

    b. well-being   **d.** honor

10. I need to _____ this into English. Can you help me?

    a. calculate   **c.** greet

    b. accuse   **d.** translate

11. His jokes aren't funny to me. I guess I don't appreciate his

    _____.

    a. disgust   **c.** humor

    b. rage   **d.** cheerfulness

12. I need to know the _____ meaning of that word. It's very important.

    a. precise   **c.** former

    b. suitable   **d.** striking

13. When you go to a job interview, it is important to dress _____.

    a. particularly   **c.** properly

    b. deliberately   **d.** artificially

14. I will always _____ the smell of that perfume with my mother.

    a. reveal   **c.** entertain

    b. focus   **d.** associate

15. That vase looks heavy, but it isn't because it's _____.

    a. domestic   **c.** hollow

    b. immature   **d.** endless

16. There is going to be a party to _____ him next week.

    a. shame   **c.** honor

    b. observe   **d.** stretch

17. Children who are learning how to read usually start by reading

    _____.

    a. out loud   **c.** eventually

    b. in contrast   **d.** out of sight

18. The price of a new car _____ from $10,000 to $40,000.

    a. backs up   **c.** flashes

    b. ranges   **d.** calculates

19. If a police officer comes to arrest you, it is illegal to _____.

    a. possess   **c.** focus

    b. analyze   **d.** resist

20. Oranges are usually sweet, but this one is very _____.

    a. contagious   **c.** suitable

    b. mild   **d.** bitter

21. He sometimes makes mistakes, but _____ he's doing a very good job.

    a. in contrast   **c.** eventually

    b. particularly   **d.** overall

22. It was a _____ that she died so young.

    a. pile   **c.** tragedy

    b. fraud   **d.** witness

23. Are you angry with him? You didn't _____ him when he came in.

    a. greet   **c.** ignore

    b. confirm   **d.** abuse

24. It is a _____ opportunity. You will never have such a good opportunity again.

    a. royal   **c.** poetic

    b. unique   **d.** mild

25. I tried to talk to him, but he completely _____ me.

    a. ignored   **c.** invested

    b. infected   **d.** reviewed

26. He is _____ to find her. He won't stop searching until he does.

    a. disgusted   **c.** puzzled

    b. reserved   **d.** determined

27. Her _____ with money is destroying her life.

    a. discount   **c.** institute

    b. function   **d.** obsession

28. I can't go on the trip. My mother won't give me _____.
    a. physicians   c. permission
    b. standards   d. requests

29. What _____ are you wearing? It smells heavenly!
    a. stains   c. legend
    b. fragrance   d. flash

30. It is a complex _____. Only an expert can explain it to you.
    a. scent   c. infant
    b. lid   d. procedure

31. The answer is _____. I don't know why I didn't think of it
    before.
    a. secretive   c. contagious
    b. proper   d. obvious

32. It feels good to _____ when you first wake up in the morning.
    a. entertain   c. slip
    b. stretch   d. gesture

33. If you _____ only on the details, you might not be able to see
    the big picture.
    a. interfere   c. possess
    b. invest   d. focus

34. Some people have a special _____ with dogs. They can almost
    read their minds.
    a. bond   c. drum
    b. tale   d. guilt

35. She's a _____ woman. Everyone who meets her remembers
    her.
    a. well-being   c. innate
    b. mild   d. striking

36. Please don't walk on the grass. Stay on the _____.
    a. theme   c. lid
    b. journal   d. path

See the Answer Key on page 256.

Vocabulary Self-Tests Answer Key

Below are the answers to the vocabulary self-tests. Check your answers, and then review any words you did not remember. You can look up words in the index on the next two pages. Then go back to the readings and exercises to find the words. Use your dictionary as needed.

Vocabulary Self-Test 1 (Units 1–3; pages 123–126)

1. b	10. c	19. c	28. d
2. b	11. b	20. c	29. c
3. a	12. d	21. c	30. a
4. a	13. c	22. a	31. d
5. d	14. d	23. a	32. b
6. b	15. d	24. b	33. c
7. a	16. b	25. c	34. c
8. b	17. d	26. c	35. b
9. d	18. c	27. a	36. c

Vocabulary Self-Test 2 (Units 4–6; pages 252–255)

1. d	10. d	19. d	28. c
2. a	11. c	20. d	29. b
3. d	12. a	21. d	30. d
4. d	13. c	22. c	31. d
5. a	14. d	23. a	32. b
6. b	15. c	24. b	33. d
7. c	16. c	25. a	34. a
8. b	17. a	26. d	35. d
9. a	18. b	27. d	36. d

INDEX TO TARGET WORDS AND PHRASES